D1603475

THE
STRONG
PLACE

The Strong Place

MARION
DUCKWORTH

Tyndale House Publishers, Inc.
Wheaton, Illinois

First printing, January 1983

Library of Congress Catalog Card Number 82-50697
ISBN 0-8423-6663-6, paper
Copyright © 1983 by Marion Duckworth
All rights reserved
Printed in the United States of America

To Jack

CONTENTS

PART ONE

1 / The Promise / 13
2 / The Choice / 23
3 / The Strong Place / 31

PART TWO

4 / Rest / 43
5 / Intimacy / 53
6 / One Thing at a Time / 63
7 / Moment by Moment (1) / 73
8 / Moment by Moment (2) / 85

PART THREE

9 / Love / 97
10 / Will / 109
11 / Prayer (1) / 123
12 / Prayer (2) / 133
13 / Fruit / 147
14 / Death to Life / 161
15 / By Faith / 173

Suggested Reading / 185

I am the true vine, and my Father is the husbandman. Every branch in me that beareth not fruit he taketh away: and every branch that beareth fruit, he purgeth it, that it may bring forth more fruit. Now ye are clean through the word which I have spoken unto you. Abide in me, and I in you. As the branch cannot bear fruit of itself, except it abide in the vine; no more can ye, except ye abide in me.

I am the vine, ye are the branches: He that abideth in me, and I in him, the same bringeth forth much fruit: for without me ye can do nothing. If a man abide not in me, he is cast forth as a branch, and is withered; and men gather them, and cast them into the fire, and they are burned. If ye abide in me, and my words abide in you, ye shall ask what ye will, and it shall be done unto you. Herein is my Father glorified, that ye bear much fruit; so shall ye be my disciples. As the Father hath loved me, so have I loved you: continue ye in my love. If ye keep my commandments, ye shall abide in my love; even as I have kept my Father's commandments, and abide in his love.

These things have I spoken unto you, that my joy might remain in you, and that your joy might be full. This is my commandment, That ye love one another, as I have loved you. Greater love hath no man than this, that a man lay down his life for his friends. Ye are my friends, if ye do whatsoever I command you. Henceforth I call you not servants; for the servant knoweth not what his lord doeth: but I have called you friends; for all things that I have heard of my Father I have made known unto you. Ye have not chosen me, but I have chosen you, and ordained you, that ye should go and bring forth fruit, and that your fruit should remain, that whatsoever ye shall ask of the Father in my name, he may give it you. These things I command you, that ye love one another.

John 15:1–17 KJV

PART ONE

THE
PROMISE
⁙

1 I sat on the sofa swathed in end-of-the-
day listening—waiting for a whisper from
God. No magazine-and-Sanka sprawl.
Upright . . . expectant . . . hoping that
any moment God's presence would brush
my spirit and shed Shekinah light on the
Bible words in my lap.

"Abide in me, and I in you" (John 15:4, KJV).
Promise of a locked-in-God life. A human/divine
meld, morning to night, morning to night.

If ever God was going to peel away the mystery
from these words, it would be at a time like
tonight. The last putting away had been completed
and the daytime mind-spin had slowed . . .
slowed. . . . Mark, bathed and pajamaed, had been
committed to the safety of God-blessed sleep. On
a windowsill, his green plush rabbit—most special
friend—sat waiting for the first morning's hug.

In the mother part of my mind I saw Paul and
John in the other bedroom. Reluctantly, Paul had
rested his guitar against one wall for the night.
From his bed, he imagined chord changes,

13

stretching and arching eleven-year-old fingers
under his covers. Finally, fingers stilled. Only the
melody continued, playing itself over and over in
his sleeping mind.

On John's desk, pieces of his fourteenth year
lay scattered: a biology book, algebra handouts, a
Funny Car model and instruction sheet, swabs, bits
of plastic. He'd sat—putting his weight against
day's end as long as he could manage—wiping a
bit of glue from parts F and G, then propping it
against the box to dry for tomorrow and part H.

The brothers had spoken nighttime fragments
from pillow to pillow. Then one spoke . . .
waited . . . and heard only soft, steady breathing.

Tomorrow at seven these sons would be
grabbing books and hunting socks and yelling *help*
into the kitchen. Tomorrow at seven our selves
would mingle again. Tonight we had separated—
my sons to pursue their dreams; I, my vigil.

Tonight Jack hadn't waited to stretch and yawn
in wedlock at eleven o'clock. "You get the back
door; I'll turn out the lights." Midplot in a ten
o'clock TV drama, he'd risen from his chair and
padded to the hallway. "I can't stay awake. You
coming soon?"

Anticipating God in the Book, I smiled good-
night. "In a little while." I laid aside the sampler
I was embroidering in the middle of a crosstitched
O, took my Bible, read, and waited soul-stilled
for God.

During other snatches of stillness on other days
during those months in 1969, I'd pondered these
enigmatic, Christ-to-disciple, John fifteen words. In
the car waiting for Jack. During my morning time

with God. "Abide in me, and I in you . . . He that
abideth in me, and I in him . . . bringeth forth
much fruit . . ." (John 15:4, 5).

I didn't doubt that these Bible words were God's
hand extended—inviting me to unite my inner man
with him in a way that I hadn't yet experienced
during my years of knowing Jesus Christ
personally. They had "God said" authority, and
I knew they applied to me.

But what was "abiding"? Was it the God-man
twining I ached for? Exactly what kind of inner
life—deeper than flesh and bone—had Jesus
promised in these last-hour words? What kind
of fruit could be brought forth?

I knew alternate translations of the word *abide*
read "live, rest, stay." But alternate translations
didn't help me understand. How could I live (rest,
stay) in Jesus Christ? *Explain yourself, God. In
concrete nouns and verbs. Give detailed do-it
instructions like the ones on John's desk.*

But the John fifteen words were from a fifth-
level reader and I was a first-level student. So
I sought a before-God, uninterrupted hush, and
prayed for Holy Spirit interpretation. For a gasp
of breath, insight. *I see it now!*

St. John's words represented all the scriptural
passages that promised the more-than-positional,
family of God relationship I ached for.

"You were called into the companionship of His
Son, our Lord Jesus Christ" (1 Cor. 1:9, Berk).

"Christ . . . more and more at home in your
hearts . . ." (Eph. 3:17, TLB).

My inner self caressed the words . . .
"companionship with God . . ." "Christ . . . at

15

home. . . ." I was a child once estranged from my Parent, now united, who could never get enough of him.

For years, I'd wanted kitchen table intimacy with God. A lifetime of hours lingering over coffee cups with the one I loved. Union, like the times Jack and I were seated across from one another in the living room reading and as if cued, we looked up and said with our eyes *we are one.*

The God within, a constant wonder.

Until age thirty I had been first verse, Genesis one. Formless. Desolate. Engulfed in darkness.

But the spirit of God began brooding over me as I filled my shopping cart with canned peas and packages of hamburger in the A&P and as my son and I nibbled the edges of our chocolate wafer ice-cream sandwiches in Woolworth's.

Genesis one, verse two. First-day creation. While the subway rumbled beneath me taking its passengers to Times Square to a movie at the Roxy and strawberry shortcake at Toffenetti's, I was kneeling before the One who spoke a universe into existence, seeking his Son. I whispered God's name and waited for him to step from beyond galaxies. *Please, God, please, God, please, God, be there.*

He was there.

While subway cars pulled into Sunnyside, doors opened, doors closed, the Christ-God moved into my world of animal cracker tigers.

Thirty, my beginning.

Days of creation continued. God the Holy Spirit tended my newly born spirit lovingly, by a process hidden within my frame—at once as mysterious and awesome to me as the Genesis one, heaven and earth creation. Elohim directed my gaze and creatures of earth became a double wonder. Sons, fingers and toes molded by God. Jimmy, our parakeet, a splash of chattering green. The tree that grew in the middle of the sidewalk on the way to the park. Upstairs and downstairs neighbors. Originals. Each revealing his brush stroke, each marked with his unmistakable sign.

I still wore the same pajamas. Brushed with the same toothpaste. Same strawberry jam on my toast. Same favorite spot on the sofa. But now I was experiencing a new longing like a second heartbeat.

Hungry. I was always hungry for more of God than yesterday. I wanted to know him more intimately, understand his nature more clearly, discover his will more completely, obey him more readily.

I studied the Bible and in spite of stumble-over names and places that I had to locate by tracing numbers and letters on the map, a verse or phrase would separate from the rest and become a line penned to me. My sons grew molars; they joined Cub Scouts. I read and studied, searched and prayed for a way deep into the cleft of the Rock.

Finger-reading the lines, I'd stop to gasp and shake my head as I gazed inward. "Rivers of living waters shall flow from the inmost being of anyone who believes in me" (John 7:38, TLB). *Rivers, Lord? Not cupfuls?*

John the apostle's *enthousiasmos* spilled out of his words and down through the centuries, as from a man filled to bursting with God. "We saw Him

17

and we heard Him and are telling you, so that you too may enjoy fellowship along with us. And this fellowship of ours is with the Father and with His Son . . ." (1 John 1:3, Berk).

Fellowship. And again: *fellowship.* More than Marion meet God. Intercourse—inner man with God. I squeezed the words until they ached.

I *wanted* that fellowship. I *wanted* to be consciously, continuously aware of God's presence in my life. I wanted an experiential, breath by breath he/me relationship with the Holy Spirit of God who lived in me.

Occasionally during my early Christian years, the Jehovah God had filled my holy of holies.

During crisis, I'd been aware that Father God was a faithful parent. Paul, waving a rattle at the world one moment and silent with burning fever like a patch of midnight sun the next. He was beyond pats or kisses or a warm bottle of milk. I felt as helpless as though I had to move a world with the power of my arms.

Dead of night desperation. I rocked, singing "Lullaby and Good-night" to the rhythm of the chair. Then, a Presence within like an arm around my soul until dawn grayed the living room window and Paul's hair lay in perspiration ringlets against his head.

When I had needed direction, there had been the silent sound of the Holy Spirit's voice. There was the time Jack was working at a job in which he couldn't honor God. "Pray about what I should do," he asked me.

As I walked to the grocery store, I prayed, "What should we do?" When I opened the bell-

clanging door and walked toward the mountain
of bread, the conviction came: "Honor me."

At midweek service a few days later, every eye
closed, every head bowed, I prayed, "What should
we do?" The conviction: "Honor me."

Alone on an evening praying walk, I asked God:
"What should we do?"

He answered, "I've already told you what to do.
Why do you ask me again?"

My words back were on their knees. "Yes, Lord.
I do know. Amen, Father."

He'd been an assuring presence when I'd sat on
Job's ash heap. A Ten Commandment authority.
The source of wisdom, of hope, of insight, of
praise in my soul when I studied Scripture and
prayed.

But why was Kingdom of God intimacy a holiday
only? How could I touch him within on Monday
morning while I ate my granola? Since God was
God and lived in me, why didn't my heart burn
within as we walked together?

Prostrate surrender followed surrender. A cool
June evening at a Bible conference. A prayer, a
song. The speaker moved from sermon point
one to two and then three. "Surrender," he
ended softly.

About a dozen of us gathered to pray. We sat
bowed, Isaiahs in the Temple. With shaking voices,
some confessed that they had segregated their
Loved One from areas of their lives. Silently, I
held out the key to every door. "I surrender."

Back home, I was still filled only with the sounds
of my own thoughts and feelings. I tried reaching
for a new surrender. *Occupy me, God,* I pleaded

19

and crawled into a corner of my life so that he
could march through.

Failure.

I would die a Romans chapter six death. "Think
of yourselves as dead, so far as sin is concerned,
but living in fellowship with God through Christ
Jesus (Rom. 6:11, TEV). Trying to understand,
I traced the passage backward through its tight
doctrinal statements, then ahead through the
eighth chapter's *live in the Holy Spirit* crescendo.
I highlighted the words with yellow, underlined
them with red, cross-referenced them and
annotated them. But they lay knotted and twisted
in front of me.

One vacation on the shore, I read Watchman
Nee's explanation of the Romans chapters in *The
Normal Christian Life.* But Nee's explanation about
the death and burial of my birthroom self was hard
and oddly shaped and wouldn't fit into my brain.
*See myself dead as far as sin is concerned, but
living in fellowship with God. . . .* The calculus of
Scripture. I felt like an illiterate caressing words
that were only black marks to my eyes.

Back home, I put Nee's book and my Bible on
the shelf and tried to die to sin—to see myself
nailed to a cross, entombed, then rising to an
everlasting Easter morning, a body full of God,
controlled by His Spirit.

But Calvary suicide in my imagination didn't
produce death. I knelt to die and rose to sin again.

I *wasn't* dead to sin. I *wasn't* experiencing
Easter morning. How many more surrenders
before that flash of insight that sent me into the
streets shouting hosannas?

20

The harder I tried to make intimacy happen—to run from the shady to the sunny side of the Christ-in-me life, the more hopeless it seemed. But the Bible promised *real* fellowship; I would comb its chapters until I found the key.

I searched other Bible writers' words, pushing on their doors for a way in. I squinted at men like Moses whom God had called "friend"—men to whom spirit was as authentic as flesh—and I longed for their secrets.

Then I found Jesus' words in John chapter fifteen. Before, it had only been the chapter between fourteen and sixteen. Now, those words were God's hand extended. Intimacy. Christlikeness. Productivity. A person-branch living in a Person-Vine.

As I sat in the living room, with my Bible on my lap, praying and listening to the fireplace crackle that night in 1969, the John fifteen words began to glow with Shekinah light, as though *spiritual* illumination had become *visible* for the sake of flesh.

In the nighttime silence, my soul pirouetted and sang its own psalm. *God promised. He promised.*

Anxious to find the place where continuing intimacy began, I ran down one path, then another. Perhaps if I located the exact spot within where God dwelled and kept myself there? I strained harder in prayer, pushed deeper inside, searching for the center of his presence.

Could I begin to live in Christ by bearing fruit? I pleaded for others' needs, claimed promises, tried to trust, and waited to fill my basket with success to give God.

21

Was it by pruning? I hacked at deadwood habits here, there, and stood straining to be promoted into intimacy. Was it by keeping my mind focused on God? I taped Scripture passages to the bathroom mirror, propped cards over the kitchen sink to repeat continuously, as though they were brainwashing slogans.

Nothing that I did made the Bible passage come true for me. I felt like Abram in Haran: "Go to a country that I am going to show you" (Gen. 12:1, TEV). Had Abram run to the outskirts of Haran searching for the way to the Promised Land only to sit frustrated by the side of the road to listen again? "Go to a country *that I am going to show you*"?

God brought Abram to Canaan and me to the place of rest in Jesus Christ.

He began by teaching me that he loved me and that *he* wanted intimacy with *me* as much as I did with *him*. I began to let him father me. Instead of living self-condemningly, he taught me to live self-acceptingly; instead of self-protectively, vulnerably.

But the creation of old-to-new Marion was no breath-into-nostrils, sixth-day event. I was still Marion-centered, like a child sitting upright on Daddy's lap, engrossed in a Marion world, thinking Marion thoughts, feeling Marion feelings. This was not John fifteen intimacy. Only after more pruning by my Father the Gardener would I learn how to lean into him, to rest, to abide.

THE
CHOICE
⋮

2 Dawn peered into our bedroom window and splashed golden patches of empty-tomb promise on the bare floor. For minutes, I turned my back and clung to dream safety. But sunlight had severed night. I squinted at day through folds of sleep.

Sunday. Which resurrection celebration? Cinnamon rolls and songs on the way to Sunday school? Chicken dinner and naps after church? Giggles and games on the floor in front of the fireplace and waffles spread with "God is good"?

Day of rest and sun-bright sky no longer fooled me into welcoming Sunday. Even its early morning edges had a sour odor.

I watched Jack sleep. My husband's eyes were shut tightly against today. He breathed. He lay motionless, not breathing. Finally, he breathed again, as though he were accepting life grudgingly. I longed to fall back on my own cushion of sleep until I could retreat into the safety of Monday.

Weekdays were ready-made regimens of twenty-

23

four hours that began with a gulp of breakfast and ended with exhaustion. *Supervisors and vice presidents; open house at school at seven; supermarket excursions.* "You get six cans of tuna; I'll get the eggs." Tomato worms, aphids on the rosebushes. But on Sunday, a day that rattled with extra hours, Jack and I lived in separate cells with thick walls of circumstances between us.

For me, the first day of the week began with terror and foxhole prayers. I counted its hours as though it were a slowed pulse, glad when I could finally wrap it in nighttime prayers and bury it under a mound of Sundays past.

I hid during those Sundays behind projects and papers and stepped from one safe topic of conversation to another. The midday meal was starched with formality: "Would you like more peas, dear?" And "I'm going to make a pot of tea. Will you have some?" Finally, formality cracked and I ran with my sobs to the garage or the bathroom or even the backyard.

Sunday had been the day when Jack stood in his pulpit and preached. The Reverend John Duckworth had been pastor to farmers and loggers in churches built on Saturday workdays with potluck lunches served from tailgates of station wagons. After an illness, he asked for a leave of absence from the missionary organization with which we served, but was advised to return to his pastorate instead. A few years later when a coronary threatened and he was unable to execute the responsibilities of a missionary/pastor in that community, he resigned.

Now he was well and ready to return. We

reapplied for a pastorate and prepared to pack
dishes in barrels and linens in boxes and load
them into a U-Haul.

But our request for a pastorate was refused.

I stared at the letter. The organization's heading
was printed in blue, family-familiar, like the
hundreds that had been dropped into our
mailboxes before it, yet not like them at all.

We read sentences aloud to one another,
then stood silent, staring at the other's face,
then through it and beyond at nothing.

"But we haven't been raising money for a
new ministry in communities we served," one
of us finally managed, speaking too loudly
as though shouting down the letter's accusations.
"And we haven't been visiting a lot of former
parishioners. . . ." Our eyes scraped heaven
for some tribunal to affirm our innocence,
to thunder vindication.

Application denied splintered our sleeping and
waking hours. It leered through Sunday in church
bells and calls to worship. *Jack will tell me that
everything's all right,* I assured myself as I knelt to
gather the pieces of our lives. But my husband was
staring through the invisible faces of wife and sons
at mind scenes that he couldn't dismiss.

This was a trouble that I couldn't kiss away. I
couldn't massage his head "like this, so you move
my scalp" and stroke away frustration with my
love. He came and went, stood, sat, and lay down
to sleep always separated from me by questions
without answers.

This couldn't have happened to us. We'd swung
hands and exchanged long, loving looks through

25

the decades of Mr. and Mrs. His favorite sayings
had become mine; my next sentence was on the
tip of his tongue. At night, we were S-shaped
figures warming one another under winter
bedcovers.

So long as we could rush from shopping to
gardening to music lessons to dental appointments
and cover ourselves with the surface sounds of
society, I could survive. But the day of pastor-in-
the-pulpit always came, when Jack reviewed our
rejection and its implications and weighed courses
of action.

Sundays were prisons in which I must spend
twenty-four hours. Tension mounted and I
pounded their walls and prayed, *Make everything
better.* But Jack and I remained like New York City
strangers seated across from one another on
the subway staring at our hands, then at the
floor, while the train roared through an endless
black tunnel.

The clock radio rasped, "Bad, bad Leroy Brown"
and I reached over and pushed rock-and-roll out of
our Sunday silence. Best clothes from hangers.
Turns in the bathroom, english muffins and jam on
the table. Sons sat, fumbling with the first minutes
of the day. They managed sentence fragments:
"Sports section . . . pants need ironing . . . peanut
butter . . . more milk."

*Are they testing our Lord's day mood with
these few words?* Do they recognize my plastic
cheerfulness as I mother?

I chased the dog off the bed and pulled up the
covers. The rhythm of pre-Sunday school routine:
bathrobes on hangers, Bible, jacket; purse on

chair, shades pulled up and lined at window's
halfway mark—a few second's tranquilizer. The
clock radio had ticked to 9:20. Blow dryers buzzed
their last few seconds and we filed down the
back steps.

But *application denied* rode with us to church. It
crowded between us on the pew. Because of its
presence, we couldn't hold hands and squeeze
fingers through the sermon or exchange secret
smiles. It had tightened our throats until we
couldn't sing bass/alto duets, a two-person choir.

Jesus, I sobbed in my soul. *Jesus.* I waited until
"Let us pray" and heads were bowed and eyes
were closed to remove my glasses and wipe the
tears. Worship had become only a church bulletin
word. I couldn't worship; I could only moan
desperation before the Throne.

Plastic mother cheerfulness crumbled by Sunday
afternoon. No longer was I able to play "Lord's
Day Let's Pretend" for the sake of the children.
Careful to seem casual. "Going out in the yard . . ."
"Guess I'll go for a walk . . ." I'd disappear to the
darkened garage behind trunkfuls of baby blankets
and first white shoes or to the bathroom where I'd
slide the bolt, turn on the water in the basin, and
retch sobs on the linoleum floor. Not dainty
Victorian tears—ugly chunks of my soul. They
were the end of the rope, beyond prayer. They
were an ultimatum in the face of God. Our future
was splintered and my husband was alienated from
me by his preoccupations and the emotions that
they generated in him. *I . . . can't . . . stand . . .
it . . . ! Do . . . something.*

I couldn't go on. I'd give up. Go to bed forever;

27

give myself to emotional collapse. Then, someone else could be strength for me again. But the sounds of sneakers outside my closed door were crib-cries grown up. They jabbed at the mother in me as they had done to women since Eve, bringing me back, startling me upright, to smear my face dry, to head for the door and help find a sweater, a library book.

Why these months of misery? I asked a Marion who had no answer. God's promise of intimacy was as remote as the stars. Instead of John fifteen abiding, branch in Vine, I was alone, crushed with the weight of my own feelings. The anxiety from all the situations I'd ever faced seemed to be swept into this one. I slipped, clawed the dirt, and slipped again.

One Sunday afternoon, I fled to our bedroom and flopped face down across the bed. As always, I'd begged God for peace to fall with the morning dew like manna and nourish me through the day. But no peace fell. Instead, I felt like a Mary, standing at the grave of my Lord, wishing him back. I sobbed anger at my own weakness, at Jack for suffering private pain, at God for his endless silence.

Tears were my final hope. They would change things. Jack would walk into the bedroom and vow to be happy ever after so that I could be happy ever after, too. God would pat me and croon, *Poor baby,* and erase this page from our lives.

I . . . can't . . . go . . . on. I sobbed to God and lay on the pink spread wet with self-pity. Then, words from the root of creation, firm with Divinity's authority: "You must go on. You can choose to go on—to stop giving in to these feelings you are experiencing."

Choose to go on? Hadn't I tried? Hadn't I prayed? Didn't I begin each Sunday with a plea that this would be a day full of "Praise the Lords"?

Choose to go on? How could I choose to go on when I was paralyzed with feelings that stiffened muscles and mind, that mixed with the blood in my veins and pulsed into chest and stomach, arms and legs, until I was weak and trembling?

How could I choose to go on? Tension still hung thick in the air. The extraterrestrial love that I needed hadn't filled me. No fold of arms had gathered me up and held me close. There was only another Sunday in which to weep myself raw and wipe away my own tears.

Choose?

I lay face down, clinging to the bed, trying to hide in a softness where hard choices wouldn't follow. With trembling sobs like aftershocks, I begged God to change his mind and speak tender Father-to-child words. But the only sounds were the clicking on of the furnace; a football play-by-play coming from the living room—and the words within: *choose to go on.*

There *was* a moment like the space between ticks of a clock when I decided that I couldn't share space with my feelings any longer—when I chose to give in.

I turned on my back and stared hard at the words. *You can*, God had said. *You can choose to go on.* But my feelings of anxiety were so powerful! The presence of God had to become stronger than my feelings and fill me with a surge

29

of spiritual energy that strengthened my resolve. Then, I could choose to obey.

You can. . . . God would not have *said* that I could refuse to give in to my feelings if I were not able to *do* it. The words were more than censure. The strength to *do* was inherent in them because of the nature of the One who had spoken.

For the first time since *application denied,* I wanted to stop begging God or Jack to make nice-nice. For the first time I wanted to find strength within to control my emotions.

On the next Sunday when I began to plan an escape to the bedroom or garage, Divinity's words stood squarely in my path. *Choose. You can choose.* Deterioration or wholeness.

Obey/disobey sides were drawn and I stood swaying in the center.

With a single, silent *help,* I sprang up, stumbled around the coffee table, past bathroom and bedroom havens, to the kitchen counter. Puppy followed, prancing round at my feet until her hind and front ends nearly met, woofing for biscuits. I pushed through panic to see her, to watch her snatch one from my hand, carry it to the rug as usual, crunch it, and return for another.

I grabbed for a piece of routine to hold on to. *Supper. Cake for dessert. German chocolate, with caramel icing.*

THE STRONG PLACE

3 I squinted at the factory directions on the cake mix box through a wash of tears, rubbed my eyes hard with the back of my hand, and squinted again. "Pull red strip to open." As though screaming with my fingers, I dug at the sliver of red tape that seemed to melt flawlessly into the wrapper. My mind was shredding the pictured chocolate layers, ripping the cardboard. . . .

But beyond the screams, in my Spirit-born self, I wanted to find the end of the red strip, to pull it deftly as though it were a Tuesday afternoon three years ago and I was baking chocolate cupcakes for a school party. Will clenched its teeth. Seconds later I saw: *there, flat against the box. The red strip.* I pulled, and the top of the wrapper separated neatly from the rest. Box and inner package opened easily.

Powdery chocolate spread across the counter as I shook the mix into a bowl and switched on the electric beater. "Forty-five, fifty seconds. . . ." Sunday panic chopped my breaths as I watched the second hand and moved the beaters in a circle around the bowl.

When the batter was thick and smooth, a son wandered into the kitchen twirling a basketball on his finger. I turned and worked a greeting across my face.

"I just broke my record," he said stepping and dodging to keep the ball balanced. When it slid to the floor, he stopped and looked at the counter. "Hey, chocolate cake? For tonight?"

"For tonight. With ice cream."

"All *right.*" He bounced the ball across the kitchen floor and down the steps.

As I greased the pans, I stepped outside of myself and listened. Terror-fire still burned within. But deep in my center was a strong place that I hadn't sensed before. Solid immovable.

I exclaimed in awe before God. Minutes before, I'd been a Job down the centuries going about in darkness without sunshine. When I chose to obey and acted on that choice, I sensed the Strong Place. *I can go on. I can obey in spite of the way I feel—because of the Strong Place.*

I slid the pan into the oven. Tonight, I'd serve chocolate cake on our good stemmed cake plate with milk in our best glasses. We'd ask God's blessing on it and eat it slowly and then go back for just a taste more.

Sunday panic was still pushing at me, begging me to escape, to heave misery. But I stood timorously on a Parent-strengthened will. *I will clean off the counter. I will wash the dishes. I will go out into the yard and watch the boys play one-*

32

on-one. I will come inside again and make seven-minute frosting.

I will win because of the Strong Place.

On another Sunday, I chose to play Frisbee on the lawn instead of weeping tears across the bed. When fear began to roll over me and pushed sobs into my throat, I walked/ran to the living room, choosing God, driven by a "want to" as strong as I'd ever experienced. Could I count on the Strong Place again? "Who wants to play Frisbee?"

Sons and I hunted among baseball hats and Ping-Pong paddles for our plastic saucer. Part of me still felt like wailing and pounding the sides of my world with my fists. But at the same time, determination was growing not to give in. With every move I made digging through balls and snorkels, I was growing more determined to obey.

Mark and I moved to opposite edges of the backyard where pitching and skimming lessons began. "Hold it like this, Mom. Stand sideways, elbow up. Straighten it out. Now, let it go easy."

I pitched the saucer; it curved and rolled on edge into the street.

"This time straighten your arms out more. Watch me." My son zipped it toward me; I leaped gracelessly to catch it. Womb seed, mother-son laughter bounced between us as the saucer fell at my feet.

I was standing in the Strong Place.

Each time, I had to choose again. Sometimes, I simply allowed misery to smother me and regressed into fear tears. Then I followed a predictable cycle: hysterics alone until I was numbed. Repentance.

Days of physical exhaustion. Acceptance again of
the facts: God wasn't going to kiss my life and
make it better. He wanted me to go on living
constructively in spite of the way I felt. When I
chose to do so, the Strong Place was greater than
my fear.

The warm joy that accompanied obedience, like
my Parent's *well done,* was reinforcing my will.
Now, when I found myself sinking into my own
dark interior, I knew that I had to believe in God's
strength waiting on the other side of obedience. I
remembered, too, the joy of pleasing my Father. *I
want to please him again.* A set of my will, a push
to act on that choice—like a deep breath before
morning push-ups—and I had stepped into the
Strong Place.

Move to the garage, but not to hide behind
trunks and sob myself dry. Grab trowel and hoe
and squat in my postage-stamp-sized garden.

Spade sun-hardened soil between the rows. Pull
weeds with the pent-up force of unshed tears. Dig
around roots deep in the ground. Grunt and sweat.

Begin to notice garden life. A green worm on a
green vine. Tomato vine smell on my fingers. Bean
tendrils wound around the tomato plants like
tangled yarn. Feel fear diminish. Live in the Strong
Place. A taste of hurrah.

Choose God and win. Each time I chose to obey
and acted on that choice—each time I pushed into
the kitchen/yard/garden made it a little easier
to do next time. Each time I pulled weeds/picked
herbs to dry/played catch made it a little easier
next time. Shaking sick, yet able to obey. Afraid,
yet unafraid. Weak, yet strong.

I was an invalid putting my weight upon the arm
of promise. "Lift up your tired hands, then, and
strengthen your trembling knees! Keep walking
on straight paths, so that the lame foot may
not be disabled, but instead be healed"
(Heb. 12:12, 13, TEV).

I was beginning to understand that runaway
anxiety couldn't be reasoned with. I couldn't shake
my finger in my own face, "See here, girl, shape
up!" Fear was simply *there,* like a specter rising
out of late night shadows.

When its Gestapo step sounded on the stair,
I stood immobilized, in fear of my own fear. But
God had shown me his way of escape: choose to
obey, act on that choice, and find his strength
there waiting.

Even when I chose to dig around the tomato
vines instead of sobbing in isolation, feelings of
anxiety didn't stop. On my knees in the dirt, the
afternoon sun on my back, I felt myself shaking
inside my own skin.

A son appeared from around the corner of the
garage. "I wondered where you were. I'm going
to play basketball at the playground."

A neighbor appeared from around the hedge.
"Look at all that ambition! Say, your tomatoes
look real good."

Each time, I turned away from the inner
trembling, vowing obedience.

Father hadn't shut up anxiety in some barred,
sound-proof inner cell where it would change
shape and slip out through a crack. From the first,
he'd made it clear that I had to stand and face
those fears in him.

35

Gradually, each time I stood on a Holy Spirit-strengthened will, those feelings diminished . . . diminished. . . . I stopped digging dirt or swishing mint leaves through cold water, stopped pulling the brush through Puppy's fur, startled. *They are gone. The fears are gone.* I worshiped within, loving my Father.

During healing, I wondered *why?* to God. Why had he allowed me to become emotionally debilitated until I behaved like my own son at four? Who was this stranger who wanted to fill the air with screams?

She was me. Marion at eleven, finally giving sound to the fears she'd pushed into a hard place in her stomach because she knew there was only thirty five cents until the relief check came. She sat on the couch across from mother, coloring a picture of a smiling girl picking flowers. Birds flew around the girl's head. Marion tried to color some of them, but pressed too hard and broke her new blue crayon and sat mourning the pieces.

The screams came from other hard places in my stomach, pressed down, piled high. Unexpressed, they'd crowded me within. One afternoon I wiped away dust in the living room and *knew.* Instead of letting God help with my can't-cope fears, I'd tried to deny their existence. *It isn't acceptable for a Christian to be afraid and anxious. Therefore, I am not afraid.*

But I *was* afraid. These were the without-God churnings of Adam outside the Garden, crouched in the shadow of the flaming sword. Since coloring book days I had been experiencing feelings like his of helplessness, aloneness, and insecurity, that had crescendoed when the door to our future had been slammed shut and I couldn't hide in Jack, my strength.

Searching through Scripture in my mind, I realized that God doesn't flay the fearful. He only speaks "Fear not," followed by a promised "I will." He had allowed the cover to be ripped away from my emotional nature so that I'd face my feelings and see that they originated in my without-God, born-and-dying nature.

Now I knew that I didn't have to let those feelings control me. I could choose to believe God's promised "I will" and live out of born-and-becoming me—that seedling Christlike Marion Duckworth.

"At the time you are put to the test, he will give you the strength to endure it, and so provide you with a way out" (1 Cor. 10:13, TEV).

I *knew* that I was reborn in Jesus Christ, that I'd never be alone or helpless again because he lived in me. Now I had to learn to respond out of that truth—to allow old feelings to die and peace and joy from the Holy Spirit to take their place.

Learning experiences followed one another. On a Sunday afternoon, Jack sat silently in his chair. I sat on the sofa, embroidering. Paul drifted into the room and dug through the newspapers spread on the floor. "Anyone seen the sports section?"

Mark followed in minutes. "I'll be riding my bike around the neighborhood." In the corner, the TV, a mechanical third person, babbled. "He swings and misses . . . sixty seconds out for this message."

Mark slammed the door behind him and Paul stretched out on the floor to read the ball scores.

37

In my soul, cellar feelings spread like a stain in the family silence.

I prayed. *God?* Then I remembered. *This is only the way my old self responds to Sunday. These are only emotions that are unsettling me. They need not control me.*

I chose. *I will obey. Act on faith that the Strong Place will be there.*

"I found the neatest book in the library." I was shaking inside and I accepted the shaking as a Marion reaction, but refused to become occupied with it. Lifting up tired hands and strengthening weak knees, I went ahead. "It has pictures of newly hatched birds without a single feather, and a Fat Dormouse asleep with his tail curled over his head. Let me show you. . . ."

I got the book and we caught our breath as we stared at skin-covered, bulging eyelids of Wrynecks and wondered what it felt like to touch their naked bodies.

We finished the book. "I'm hungry for popcorn. Anyone want to help me make some?" The son who was family popcorn specialist volunteered. As we waited for the oil to heat in the bottom of the popper, we tried to decide whether to make one panful or two. "I can eat a bowlful myself, especially if it has lots of butter on it," he boasted.

Because I hadn't been paying attention to the panic, I realized that it had become more and more subdued, like an obstreperous child whose tantrums have gone unrewarded.

Later our bowls sat next to the sink with a few unpopped grains left in the bottom. I searched through the titles in the bookcase for C.S. Lewis or

perhaps Hannah Hurnard. Book chosen, I plumped
up the brown pillow in a corner of the couch and
settled, shifting as Puppy would, feeling the way
her face looks when, tongue out, tongue in,
she sighs.

As I read the sentences slowly, squeezing the
words of meaning, I was a wonder to myself.
Instead of anxiety, warm joy. Born and becoming.
I praised between pages.

PART TWO

REST

4 I stepped into months still chilled by *application denied* on *I will.* With a son I walked across Hickory and down Cherry. "That game against Superior Tires last week. . . ." "How's the class with that professor you told me about?" A series of commitments to "lift up your drooping hands and strengthen your shaky knees; step out straight ahead with your feet, so that which is lame may not be dislocated but rather be healed (Heb. 12:12, 13, Berk). Reaching out less often to Jack to steady me; trusting strength within instead. Allowing Jack to be healed at his own pace, while I was healed at mine.

The early question, "Would the Strong Place be there next time?" was a doubt that was melting at the edges. Inner Shekinah *was* behind the layers of old me. So long I had been in the wilderness at Kadesh, a grasshopper before giants, listening to chorused fear: "The land . . . devours its inhabitants" (Num. 13:32, Berk). Now finally, I was believing the other: "Let us confidently go up and conquer" (Num. 13:30).

On Monday mornings, I whispered a grateful *Thank you, Lord* for escorting me through another foreign Sunday and dug into the work week with both hands. There *were* times that I wanted to weep during bare spots in my six-day work week routine when I'd finished one chore and hadn't started another. Instead, I seized a job to be done in one hand and an appointment in the other—weekday weapons against disintegration—and ran a marathon toward someday.

One typical run-and-do weekday morning I stood at the sink washing one of many family somethings, thinking out of a brain in panic, rubbing, scraping with my fingers and staring, with my eyes, seeing only a faucet-porcelain blur. *Mold on the shower tiles . . . long-sleeved shirt . . . Aunt Elizabeth . . . lawn mower . . . telephone call . . .* words, words, roaring, roaring. . . .

Some sound (furnace clicking on?) or motion (car passing?) or internal nudge (God?) startled me conscious. "Listen to yourself." . . . *builds bodies eight ways . . . dinner tonight . . . bridge over troubled water . . . .* I listened, shocked, to the sound of my own thoughts. *Nothing, nothing,* I vowed. *No words, no words.* But they only pushed by.

During the next weeks, someone pulled me outside myself to listen. Again and again.

Each time I realized that mobs of words were elbowing their way through my mind, bruising as they went. They were city street strangers who

trampled one another, stomping carelessly on ends
of sentences, interrupting one another like spoiled
children. Fragmented thoughts, wounds of a
fragmented life; words born and unborn. My inner
mind rattled like a never-ending card game in the
back room. Up front over the din, I carried on
business, but always occupied within as though
I were wearing my face backward.

I couldn't rest. I wanted my world to wrestle as
I did: the houses, the yard, the grass and trees to
twist and moan so I'd feel at home. I wanted to
scratch at the suburban quiet that spread across
the lawns in my neighborhood and coated the
streets, for it seemed to come like vapor out of the
screen doors and partly raised windows from the
lives of people within and grate on my discordance

I visualized them seated across from each other
at their breakfast tables, these contented neighbors.

"Do you think we should prune the trees this
weekend?"

"The roses were lovely this year, weren't they?"

"Next spring, a patio. . . ."

They spoke too calmly to one another. They
dusted their dining rooms with soft flannel and
thought about nothing except the luster of the
wood. They built shelves in their garages,
measuring carefully, making a pencil line,
and thinking only about inches and feet.

Under pressure, I had always internalized. When
I was newly married, I'd practiced "figuring things
out" while I combed my hair, walked to the bus,
rode to work and up in the elevator. And
convinced that *no one wants to hear what I have*

to say; safer to run it around in the brain than out the mouth, the practice became a habit that intensified under stress.

I wanted my mind back. I wanted to be free to think *God here. God in me. Father, my Father.*

I fumbled for the off button: every wall of my mind was slick. No button; not even a recessed switch. Except for rare moments when my thoughts were totally focused, as during the winning moments on Sunday in the Strong Place, the cacophony continued.

One of the times when I was nudged or startled to "come inside and listen," I remembered other words. I took them out from where I had stored them like an unfinished project and examined them again.

How long had it been since I first heard them? Two years? More? It had been a hot summer afternoon a few months after Jack had resigned his pastorate and what-to-do worries were crowding my mind until my brain seemed to have become a word factory gone awry. I walked/ran to the backyard and lay in a lawn lounge to escape. I would recapture memories of pure peace when I was sixteen and lay on a beach blanket, sun-sopped and still-minded.

As I lay drenched with light and heat on my square foot of peace, the words began to melt. Sounds that words had obscured—a jay squawking in the apple tree, trucks rumbling loads to Houston and Las Vegas, a child shrieking to another, a bark, a mew—began to fringe my snatch of silence. I dreaded the end of my moment when the sun started to scorch or a son called to "come

46

and see" and the chaos of words began again.

Sinking and bobbing, I called to the Elohim of creation. *Help. Please help.*

The One who created spoke silently, "Do one thing at a time."

Why such secular-sounding words from God Almighty, Creator of heaven and earth? Why not a Bible verse suddenly made clear by the Holy Spirit? Why not an Isle of Patmos vision of the Faithful and True with a sword from his mouth to slay the words?

"Do one thing at a time." Were these unbiblical words a key to mind-peace? How? I sat straight up on the lounge chair. That these words were from God, I had no doubt. But how could "doing one thing at a time" give me a new mind?

During the months ahead, I circled the backyard God-words as though they were strangers in my jungle, and tried to obey. *Wash the dishes and then put the meat on to brown and then sit down and make out the shopping list instead of browning the meat while you wash the dishes, dripping suds from sink to stove, and stopping to add things to the list, angry because the pen won't write on the paper you wet with soapy hands.*

I couldn't obey. I tried and failed. Tried and failed. And finally stopped trying.

But I hadn't tossed God's injunction in memory's back closet under a lesson on mouth-to-mouth resuscitation and the words to a margarine commercial so that I had to scratch my head: *What was it God told me to do that afternoon? Let's see . . . I was in the lounge chair. . . .* His words hadn't been a coffee hour fancy or a self-

47

prescribed cure. I had stored them so that they'd
be ready to take up as soon as I knew how.

Now I tried to take them up again. The
Thanksgiving cactus bloomed pale pink buds and
snow tipped the rhododendron leaves and I tried to
do one thing at a time. Chickadees perched on the
swaying feeder and squirrels dug walnuts from the
flower bed and I tried. And kept trying.

But God's "one thing at a time" was an outsized
coat into which I never seemed able to grow. *I've
filled out enough now,* I'd think. *I'll try it again.* But
each time I had to let it fall to the floor, step out of
it, and back into the old ways.

My mind was monarchistic. It *gave* orders, it did
not *take* them, and doing one thing at a time was
not of its choosing. Unless I learned how to control
my thoughts, I'd never be able to do one thing at a
time. Unless God interceded, how could I control
my thoughts? The harder I worked for self-control,
the more tenaciously my mind persisted in
dominating my life.

One afternoon each week I caught a bus to the
public library. Since little girl days when I sat at low
tables on a me-sized chair and held Laura Ingalls
Wilder in my hands, libraries had been my special
place. They had a quietness that reminded me of
Grandpa's woods. Even now I set books down
carefully so they wouldn't thud, as though mother
were still at my elbow, finger to lips, cautioning.

The library was nonthreatening. Here were no
confrontations to anticipate. Books were well-
mannered; they stayed in their places on the
shelves in neat alphabetical rows and kept their
words contained between thick covers. With

books there were no relationships to maintain
or mourn; they had no egos to soothe, no feelings
to understand.

I was a figure painted into Thursday afternoon
along with students who thumbed the card
catalogue and the poor-visioned who stood reading
titles in the large print section. I read a few pages,
took a drink at the fountain, read a few pages
more, ate a Lifesaver, glanced out of the window.

I browsed Religion 200 . . . Poetry 811 . . .
Psychology 150 . . . and self-help. Always self-
help. Books with authoritative titles and slam-on-
the-desk subtitles. Ten rules; fifteen steps.

I took home armloads of them, but finally
self-help seemed to have become an idea cloned
and I moved on.

Along with knee-high leather boots, methods of
meditation and relaxation became vogue. In "New
Books," volumes on those subjects began to
appear. I read transcendental meditation hard
cover and paperbacked. *Smacks of eastern
religion,* I decided, and returned the books
before due date.

Back to browsing the aisles again. Da Vinci.
Organic Gardening. *Foxfire.* Gandhi. How to Relax.

In the aisle between bookshelves, at the
checkout desk, at the bus stop, in my seat swaying
through traffic, I flipped through *How to Relax* for
the single socko solve-it statement. At home, I
propped the book open on the kitchen table a safe
distance from the butter dish and jelly jar while
I practiced housewifery and on the toilet tank while
I set my hair.

The author was a doctor with no religion to sell.

I read through "Reasons Why People Become
Tense" to "What to Do About It." Relax away
the tension stored in your body, he stated,
and you will achieve a quiet mind. I shivered
with anticipation.

How to begin: Lie on your bed in a comfortable
position, and starting with your feet, let each part
of your body go limp in turn. Gradually upward,
day by day, shoulders, neck, head . . . mind. . . .

The only people I'd known who lay down
midafternoon had been my Grandpa, fragile,
past-middle age women, and men who wore
suspenders over their undershirts and never
worked. *Just once,* I promised myself. *Not long.*
With the book open at my side, I lay on top of the
pink chenille bedspread and began. *Toes limp. Let
them go. Now, feet, hanging on the ends of my
ankles. Sagging. Legs, heavy on the bed. . . .*

My feet did begin to feel as though a stream
trickled from toe to toe and was moving upward.
Seashore stillness traveled through my
bloodstream and into my lower legs. But my mind
raged against this midday obscenity and pulled
body strings taut. I snapped the book shut, sat up,
and put on my shoes. *No time for this.*

A few days later, I was back on the bed, book at
my side. This time I relaxed from toes to middle;
later in the week from toes to shoulders. Before
the book was due, I'd sunk in/gone limp from toes
to head. Each time was a snatch of sun and sand.

Inevitably each time, though, my mind would
roar, *Waste of time. This can't be from God. Too
secular.* Intimidated, I dropped the book in Return
where it was buried beneath Agatha Christie and

browsed further on the shelves for a few hours'
escape into a word world. How to Quilt . . .
Battered Wives . . . The Story of Glass . . . of Ants.

Another *How to Relax*. This one was slick-
covered new, with only one or two due dates
stamped inside. It had been written by a doctor
like the first. Mine for three weeks.

This doctor didn't insist that I lie down to
practice relaxation. I could do it sitting in a chair in
a comfortable position, eyes closed, concentrating
on the sound of my own breathing, naming each
breath "one," "one," to focus my mind.

Very casually, I sauntered to a chair. *Guess I'll
take a few minutes out* and picked up a magazine.
I stared at an advertisement, flipped a page and
stared at another. When I had myself off guard,
I let my body go limp. *Sag; inhale slowly, body
dripping like melting butter. Inhale; exhale . . . one.*
Thoughts gathered in protest. *Inhale; exhale . . .
one. Again.* Seconds of inner stillness.

Time up. Experiment over. Book away.

The next block of days I lived out of worry,
run-and-do habit. Finally, starched with tension
I returned to the green chair for a snatch of ease
with born-and-dying begging *no.*

I will. Sag . . . breathe . . . and for tiny parcels
of seconds the words in my brain settled like dust.

Success bred boldness. *More. . . .* Third helping,
fourth of relaxedness. Chair moments becoming
patches of peace.

Heresy, from the nail-biting part of me. *God
does not use secular library books to heal his
children.*

But from the place beyond my mind, a sixth-sense knowing: God did want me to learn to relax my body. A shocking, dare-to-believe: God among the secular! Confidence in that knowing compelled me back to the chair to go limp . . . to sink in . . . to rest.

INTIMACY

5 As dust-sized cactus seeds grew into spiny nubs in pots on the kitchen windowsill and the hen and chicks begun from a mother and her two children multiplied into a nurseryful of babies in the front yard, I practiced relaxation. Between pages three and four of a magazine assignment, after I returned from an appointment and before I started dinner, I let tension seep into the chair cushions. Minutes in the green chair lengthened to five . . . six. . . .

More and more the practice of relaxation was becoming my automatic response to born-and-dying tension. When I walked through the house and became conscious of thoughts crowding my head, I relaxed them away. In line at the bank I rested into the carpeted floor.

I'd been practicing relaxation for months the afternoon I pushed away from the manuscript I'd been working on and moved into the kitchen for workday, phase two. Dishes to dry. Laundry to fold. Which first?

Puppy lay stretched out, head on paws, in the kitchen doorway waiting for me to pick up her dish from the floor and pile it with Blue Mountain chicken, liver, and egg. At eye contact, she waggle-waggled anticipation. *Friends first,* I thought.

She ate. I zipped on my jacket, buckled the leash around her neck, and braced myself for her inevitable yank down the steps. Across the street we stopped while she sniffed Neighbor Brown's lawn. She strained us on to the border of the next yard where she stopped and sniffed again. Drizzle moistened our faces and coats and lay on the fuzz around her nose. When I giggled and bent to examine it more closely, she wagged politely as though mumbling a preoccupied remark over her shoulder.

Anticipating the next sniff, she pulled me into long strides toward the railroad tracks. A blue jay swooped and screeched and I stood and watched him perch in a tall pine while she nosed a patch of grass. A siren wailed in the distance. A dachshund yapped from a front step and then waddled into the empty street, yipping around the edges of his territory. I challenged his ferocity with a "Hey, boy" invitation for friendship that he answered by running a yapping retreat into the sanctuary of his yard again. Puppy continued her nose-to-ground sniffing exploration of the grass and gravel beside the railroad yard unconcerned, and I marveled at the ways of dogs.

Around another corner, we stopped at a vacant lot while Puppy buried her nose in the grass here and here, strained to go farther into the weeds and stopped again. In those seconds we were

54

separated by kind, dog and man, she in a world
of scents, me standing outside waiting, left to busy
myself in my own human being world.

Blue sky I thought. *A puff of white cloud.*

My senses sharpened at a stillness like the
moment at the end of a sigh. *What?*

*It's the setting. "Our Town" with the actors
offstage. It's because no one is on the streets and
the neighborhood sights and sounds belong only
to Puppy and me.*

I listened again. It was more than neighborhood
peace on a sunny afternoon, with dog and me
investigating our turf. It was more than peace *out
there.* It was peace *in here,* coming out from inside
me so that I was hearing and seeing differently.

I turned inward so that I could monitor the
sounds of my mind. *Stillness. That was it.* I hadn't
been walking and worrying down the streets
reliving this morning and anticipating this evening,
mindless of my environment. My body hadn't been
starched stiff, my mind in dialogue with itself.

But this was more than the stillness of end-of-
the-battle calm. The next moment I knew: *I was
sensing God's presence.* I was standing on the
corner of Hazel and Locust in front of a vacant lot
on a weekday afternoon conscious that Jehovah
God was at home in my spirit.

I wanted to twirl and skip down the empty
streets. I wanted to pick a handful of weeds, throw
them into the air, and let them fall into my hair.
I wanted to run with Puppy, to "arf" back at her.
To grab heaven and hug it.

Puppy strained at the leash, anxious to nose
ahead. I smiled at the house faces as we passed

55

them and howdied a fellow suburbanite who was sloshing suds on his car. I marveled to God over a lush wandering jew that hung in the car washer's living room window, and laughed in God's presence over a gawky setter who bounded toward us, froze in play position, and bounded again.

What were those pale orchid flowers? And orange-centered daffodils? Had I ever seen those before?

I gave Puppy the lead and stretched my stride to match hers as we rounded the corner toward home. A patch of marigolds, a border of nasturtiums . . . yellows, pinks, purples, greens blending with greens. As we sailed past, I spread these before God as a thank offering and in my spirit I sang a jubilee: *Glory be to you, Father, and to your Son . . .*

And to the Holy Ghost. In the front door. "Didn't we have fun, Pup?" as I unleashed her. She answered: waggle, waggle.

To the desk. I took out my journal, a green loose-leafed notebook salvaged from Mark on a last day of school. Using my own form of speedwriting, I put down an account of the walk. Part of me was afraid that this sense of God would be gone with the next moment. *Give it form and substance. Reduce it to concrete nouns and action verbs.*

When I had finished, I closed the notebook and sat back in my chair. Could it be that I was sitting in every day at my scarred desk behind smudged bedroom walls with dust balls on the floor and paper heaped in the wastebasket, conscious of God's presence in me?

I touched the cold metal of the typewriter table, but that didn't change my consciousness of him, the joy and peace in my spirit. I moved my back against the chair, my feet on the floor. Contacts with the material world didn't change my inner state.

This is God living in me. This was Scripture become experience, the union described by John: "I shall ask the Father and He will give you another Helper to stay with you forever. . . . You know Him, for He remains with you and will be within you" (John 14:16, 17, Berk). Fellowship during the age of the Holy Spirit was just as real as during the incarnation of the Son.

I went back to the kitchen to resume five o'clock chores. An ant ran across the countertop; I squashed it under a finger and washed the body down the sink. The phone book had been left lying in a puddle of water by the last caller. It was soggy to its XYZ pages. I looked out of the window above the sink and was reminded that no one had mowed the lawn yet, and the sky was clouding for rain.

The phone jangled and the voice on the wire rose and fell as though the speaker was dragging his words up and down a mountain. "Problem, problem," he said. "Problem. Problem."

A door slammed. A family member walked in, without even a "What's for supper?" I loaded the washing machine and remembered that I'd forgotten to call the insurance agent. The office was closed.

I panicked. Somewhere between that ant and the insurance agent, my consciousness of God had faded. *Could* I fellowship with God here where birds don't sing and squirrels don't scamper? Could a suburban writer-housewife in tennis shoes with a hole in the toe actually experience intimacy with God on earth? Or was I creating a spiritual fantasy world, an inner Nice-Nice Kingdom into which I could retreat from Nasty-Nasty? Sanctified escapism? Bluejeaned mysticism? Was I trying to duplicate the experiences of sixteenth-century saints whose paperbacked pilgrimages I had lived vicariously?

Perhaps I had been presumptuous. Perhaps intimacy with God was meant for prayer and worship times and as special surprise gifts from him. Perhaps mine had been a puny creature brashness like calling God by his first name.

I stood still in the center of the room. *No.* Intimacy with God isn't a subjective emotional experience that I need to stalk and poke at suspiciously before I can stamp it VALID. It is the natural inner state of one in whose spirit God lives. It is Eden restored.

I remembered: *Relax. Rest.* I let my shoulders sag, my arms grow heavy as though water were running through them. My fingers tingled; the tips throbbed. Physical, mental, and emotional tension began to ease and fade. *Rest, Marion Duckworth. You are living in the presence of God. He is in you.*

In deep within, I sensed him. Just *there.* Not speaking or convicting. Rest had allowed me to become conscious that Deity abided in me.

During the months after, I fellowshiped and doubted that fellowship could be valid. I was a commoner in the Palace eyeing the throne, disbelieving the King's invitation, telling myself that I'd made a terrible error. "Abide" couldn't have been meant for me.

One afternoon I sat at my desk, the painted rock paperweight and the papers it held pushed back in a corner, the chain reference Bible, exhaustive concordance, and notebook spread out in front of me, doing research for a manuscript on the subject "fellowship with God." For those hours, only the invisible Kingdom of God world had existed for me. But an ache in my legs and in the middle of my back begged movement. I circled the room, then opened the door to the hallway—and smacked into visible and tangible reality. Ugly dented and scratched filing cabinet. Scarred dresser layered with paint and missing a knob. Cases of Jack's photo equipment stored in a corner because there was no other place. Into my cracked, smudged, chipped lower middle-class world.

This is your real world. Plaster and plastic and genuine imitation leather. Fleas on the dog and ants on the counter. You are plain person Duckworth. Not a contemplative monastic living in holy solitude like one of your paperbacked saints. How can you expect to experience intimacy with God? It isn't humanly possible!

I hurried to get ahead of the words, bedroom to hallway to living room. In the center of the living room I stopped, breathed in, then out, slowly, resting in wordless communion before God. Truth had become my experience again.

"Correct," I told my rationalizing self. "I am plain person Duckworth. Polyester pantsuits with pulls. A 'now I obey God, now I don't' relationship. No

Time magazine woman of the year here. No aura of holiness lingering like Chanel #5. No isolated contemplative. Just a fiftyish woman who lives by the sweat of her brow and reeks of commonness.

"But Jesus Christ sanctified commonness. The carpenter from Nazareth, remember? He got calluses on his fingers and dirt on his robe. God in flesh who had to cut his toenails. And always, whether pounding nails or cleaning fish, living face to face with his Father.

"Of course, intimacy with God isn't humanly possible. Through no plan of mine could I initiate it. But God has. He originated the idea of Vine/ branch intimacy. The Holy Spirit speaks of it clearly in the Bible. Here: 'We saw Him and we heard Him and are telling you, so that you too may enjoy fellowship along with us. And this fellowship of ours is with the Father and with His Son Jesus Christ' (1 John 1:3).

"And here: 'That through faith the Christ may dwell in your hearts, that you may be rooted and grounded in love . . . so that you may be filled up to the whole fullness of God' (Eph. 3:17, 19). The Kingdom of God is a reality too."

I sat down and laid the Bible beside me. *Two realities.* During Jesus Christ's transfiguration when Moses and Elijah had appeared and talked with Jesus, Peter, James, and John experienced two realities. There on the mountain they saw the two worlds that exist simultaneously. Human and divine. Temporal and eternal, side by side.

Two realities. The Kingdom of the Spirit of God within and the world of fleas and ants without. I bent to Puppy who sat at my feet begging to be

scratched. "Two worlds," I told her brown eyes.
"One of inches and feet and pounds and ounces
that are dented, scarred, cracked, and chipped.
The other—the eternal one: Christ in me and
I in him."

ONE THING
AT A TIME

6 I sat upright on the edge of the sofa and looked around the room. My own outer reality: books, logs piled in front of the fireplace, a coffee table, a rocker, an afghan. Human being things that filled the space around me.

There were animate things as well. A dog. Plants. Outside the window, neighbors. In my mind, a husband and sons in the chairs and on the floor. My world.

But another world existed in this room. The *zoe* within me, the life of God in my spirit.

I got up and walked slowly around the room, pausing at a table, a bookcase, the beanbag chair in which the dog had curled up. Fur, plastic, wood, metal. I bent to touch Puppy. *Fingers against fur.* One world: visible, tangible, sensory. The other, God in my spirit, hidden like the Shekinah in the innermost part of the temple.

Puppy flipped on her back and I stroked the soft, white fur on her stomach. *With my flesh I pet the dog; in my spirit, I fellowship with God.*

I stood up and checked my watch. After three. I had to get a manuscript Xeroxed, get to the bookstore . . . As I headed out of the room, other outer world urgencies caught the corner of my eyes. *Moisture collecting on the windowsills. The jade plant needs repotting.*

Days grew into more days in which the things that could be weighed and measured grabbed at my senses, insisting that they were the true realities of life, wholly occupying my attention. Instinctively, I responded, working my way down the list of today's chores. *Manuscripts . . . meals . . . plan tomorrow.*

But sometimes, while I was quietly busy filling my place in the physical world, perhaps rubbing with soft cloth and polish, God the Holy Spirit drew me within. During those times, my spiritual sense was more compelling than my physical ones, the inner reality more compelling than the outer. "See?" God would press into my spirit. I polished with my hands and understood with my spirit and bowed in awe because truth was becoming more clearly defined, and because for those moments, inner reality was more tangible than outer.

Because the Tutor who had created me knew that I perceived truth slowly, he taught slowly. At first, he continued to affirm our relationship. One afternoon after mowing the lawn, I began sweeping the driveway of freshly mowed grass. Clumps of it stuck to the cement. I pushed at it with short, hard strokes. *Intimacy with God. Here. Now. In me.*

I picked up a stick and heaved it into the gutter. *God is here in me as I perform the commonplace activities of my life.* Whether I was sweeping the

64

driveway or brushing my teeth or involved in any
of the other insignificancies that crowded my days,
God lived in me.

I dusted our hundreds of books—front and
back covers, across, down and across the sides,
remembering fondly the pieces of my life that they
represented. Our sons' *Bible Story Reader. Halley's
Bible Handbook,* our first study help. As I picked
up others, Light rose from my spirit where he
lived, to illuminate yesterday.

Out of memory's store, the past months floated
into my conscious mind. Titles I dusted, blurred.
*You had to allow my from-the-womb, can't-cope
emotional nature to become nonfunctional, didn't
you, Lord? So I'd take a good look at it and agree
to let it die. You haven't been asking me to learn
one or two new emotional habits. You've been
asking me to "rid myself of that old nature itself
with its previous habits . . . and be renewed in my
mind and put on the new nature that is created in
your likeness . . ." (see Eph. 4:22-24, Berk).*

*Another time I walked past a house where an
orange cat lay curled up on the front step. "Your
house, kitty?" I asked its sleeping face. A block or
so later, pleased at the sight of a vivid green lawn,
neatly clipped, I thought gratitude to the strangers
in the house. "Thank you, neighbors. Seeing your
yard makes me feel good."*

Then a tug from within. I caught my breath:
*each thought has a beginning and an ending
and there are long silent spaces of mental peace
between. I am learning a new, quiet, more
controlled way of thinking, Lord. You are
doing this in me.*

This coming to see was like a months-long dawn. Light illuminated my spirit, waited for me to see, then illuminated some more. I stood at the window on a rainy afternoon and pinched leaves from a jade plant. *I see now why I haven't been able to sense your presence. The sounds from my own anxiety and self-preoccupation have been so intense that they obscured your still small voice. But you have been there, waiting.*

I could see now that physical relaxation was one of the tools God had used to pry loose born-and-dying's grip—to melt away tensions and still my thoughts so that I could know and depend on God in me. He hadn't introduced me to the relaxation technique just so I'd feel better. Relaxation was a way to introduce the idea of rest into my life. To let body, mind, and emotions know *this is what faith feels like.*

Anyone could learn to relax, but born-again ones could rest wholeheartedly because they know that God is in residence and in control of their lives. I had known that intellectually; now I was learning it experientially. Relaxation was an illustration, an introduction to the corresponding inner state of rest—leaning into, trusting implicitly in God the Holy Spirit—and was based on the principles revealed in Scripture.

From talking to myself about his presence when I was at rest, I began to talk to him as the present one more frequently. *I can trust and be at rest in spite of the pressures from the outer reality because you are at home in me. At this moment, I know that, Lord. Thank you.*

I could see that God meant for me to experience whole person rest—body, soul, and spirit. That was the kind of rest that Jesus talked about when he said "Come to Me all you who labor and are heavily burdened, and I will give you rest. Take My yoke upon you and learn of Me, for I am gentle and humble of heart and you will find rest for your souls" (Matt. 11:28, 29, Berk).

One faceless day at the height of these early faith/rest times I stood at the sink scraping garbage from a meal into the compost pail, then wiped the counter. I turned on the faucets and watched water run into the dishpan. A squirt of bubbles like handfuls of Christmas spread to the edge of the red dishpan. I plunged my hands into the water and felt warmth tingle my fingers. A cylinder of bubbles seemed to stand on hind legs and wait for my applause.

I sponged and rinsed blue and gold china, a gift from a former parish. Then the tall plastic glass Grandma had sent from New York—the one Jack drank iced tea from in summer. The coffee mug Mark gave me at Christmas. The silver, a gift from a friend.

I stopped to frown at some undefinable oddity. Then, from deep within, Light interpreted and I knew: *I am doing one thing at a time.*

I was doing dishes in the presence of God. Not doing two things at once—hands working on automatic, mind picking at a problem. Doing one thing at a time—here at the sink, seeing, feeling in the presence of God.

I washed a butcher knife. *Rusted.* How long

67

had I washed it, unseeing, because I was obligated within? I scrubbed with steel wool until I could read its mark: Case XX483-8.

Cherished chipped china and plastic glasses to tend like shrubs in Eden. An isolated moment of being alive to God, seeing and appreciating his things, hearing only the sounds of peace. His Spirit filled mine and we sang victory.

I carried trays of plants to the same sink that day for their weekly watering. *Use cold water; no time to run warm,* deep mind scowled. *You've got to visit in the nursing home in twenty minutes.* Then, I remembered and turned to God and away from those thoughts. *I am in your presence, Father God. I trust you for later on.*

I went on to wash a heart-shaped leaf, then fingered new shoots of an ivy searching for a place to wind. Notch-edged, hairy begonia leaves, jagged cactus, fans of palm, fat succulent jade. . . . I took a deep breath that was a wonder-prayer of thanks for third-day growing things, and for the fact that faith/rest was freeing me to wash and water in the presence of God. Doing one thing at a time was an everyday, jeans-and-tennis-shoes way to fellowship.

But I found that I was like a child learning to walk—tottering, falling, resorting to hands-and-knees crawl. I felt disappointed and guilty. How could I ever learn to do each task in the presence of God? The activities of life were too profuse, too varied, and so many of them demanded full mental concentration. How could I apply my mind to them and to God's presence?

I *needed* my mind to function in this world. I couldn't give my attention moment after moment

to the Holy Spirit. Was I twisting the way into a
kind of biblical mysticism?

I knew that I was not twisting the way. The
Scriptures promised fellowship with God *now.*
The times when I was able to work Spirit-filled
were earnests that kept me believing: kingdom
intimacy *was* possible.

On another work day, I sat at my desk
examining and rejecting a sentence and composing
another. From the other side of the wall I heard
the swish-rattle-whir of the washing machine slow
to click-click, bump-bump, end of cycle.
Reluctantly, I halted the parade of words, pushed
back from my desk and went to the utility room.

Smiling at sons, father, and mother pressed into
a spin-dry garble, I peeled clothing from the sides
and bottom of the washer. I separated us into
Mark's jogging socks, Jack's handkerchiefs,
everyone's underwear and towels, then loaded
the piles into a yellow basket and went down
the back steps into the yard.

With a strip of outgrown Colorado State T-shirt,
I wiped cobwebs threaded to the clothesline,
bending and ducking to see them glisten in the
sun. The biggest, thickest towel first, a blue one,
gift from the Bible class I taught. I straightened the
border and loved my Thursday morning ladies.

Socks: one green-cuffed; the other blue-cuffed.
I giggled remembering Paul as he stood in
the middle of the kitchen holding them up.
"Somewhere there's another pair just like it."
I stepped back and looked at family feet clipped
to the line.

White jogging shorts ("Two miles today, Mom").

69

I gave the clothesline a carnival spin. Was the sun shining more brightly than any other Friday morning, defining my world more clearly than I remembered seeing it before? Why this snuggled-down contentment at hanging out the laundry in a yard full of dandelions and crabgrass?

Immediately, I knew. I was hanging laundry in the presence of the Father, doing one thing at a time. Only here at the clothesline, quiet within, seeing, hearing in intimacy with God. Out of praise for grace, I twirled the clothesline again. *I am standing on a rented square of earth in a single moment separated from all others before and after it, doing my work out of my union with God.*

The rare beauty of other moments during those months when I worked out of union with God strengthened my resolve to continue learning to do one thing at a time in God's presence. Instead of thinking about doctor bills while I made the bed, I loved Jack with thanksgiving before God as I fluffed his pillow fat the way he liked it and divided covers evenly for our mock fight: *my side; your side. You have my share.*

Another day I spread vegetables on the cutting board and saw crisp orange carrots, deepest green celery stalks, cabbage leaves that curved like bowls. *I am creator, small "c," Lord, made in your image. Together we will create a Renoir minestrone for dinner for the ones we love.* These minutes had no afterward.

I walked into the bathroom and into another of these moments on an afternoon when I gave Puppy a bath. With extra towels on the floor to soak up the splash, dog soap on the toilet tank,

and pieces of cheese to feed her while we waited
for the flea-killing lather to work, I was ready.

I scooped up the shivering dog and lowered her
into the warm water. For seconds, my mind pulled
me inward. *Remember the list of phone calls to
make?* But I turned away from born-and-dying
to God the present one and rested in him.

While Puppy and I waited for the lather to work,
I fed her bits of cheese and we talked about nasty
old baths and bad biting fleas. She thanked me
with her eyes and chomped another bit from
my cupped hand, then licked it clean.

As she ran down the hall into the living room,
shaking water everywhere then speeding and
skidding onto the kitchen linoleum, I thought:
What have I been missing, turning inward? How
many leaves have turned red gold on the maple
tree outside the kitchen window? How many birds
have floated past? How many spiders have spun
webs before my eyes? I felt ravenous to experience
life in the presence of God, to be Father's child,
turning life over and over in my hand, smiling
into his face at each discovery.

Until now, I had supposed that in order to
become a Christian whose heart was set on
the things that are in heaven, I must view the
paraphernalia of earth with saintly disinterest.
Things were to feed the body, to provide shelter
from heat and cold. Keep them scrubbed clean,
replace them with plaid or plain when they wear
out. Become occupied with color, form, and
texture? Worldliness! Sin!

Not so. In the beginning, God created a man
able to touch, to listen, to taste, to feel. Peaches

were fuzzy; bark was rough. Sun felt hot and made him sleepy. Water was cold and shocked him awake.

Adam and I had been created sensuous creatures to delight with God in his world. To praise for mountain heights and cedars of Lebanon; for purple socks and Meissen porcelain, from breath to breath to breath.

MOMENT
BY
MOMENT
(1)

7 On a sunny afternoon, I pushed the mower the length of the lawn. *Even. Careful not to leave tufts of grass like a homemade haircut.* Up an incline pushing and grunting, proud to feel midlife muscles tighten on command. A glance at the mowed strip coming from my own hands and I swelled with vestigial ancestor feelings like a pioneer clearing my homestead.

Careful of the rosebush (how many weeks have you been growing there in your corner producing tiny new leaves obediently?) and of the petrified wood and crystallized rocks that lined a flower bed, pieces of back country become our own. I gentled the machine around clusters of pink rhododendron blooms (later I'll come back and touch the petals) past the front step, straddling lawn and sidewalk with the wheels. My eyes swept the clean line ahead that seemed to me to have been made with a straight edge, then over the close-cropped green squares and rectangles of order out of which my house grew.

I circled around the trunk of the japanese plum tree and the mower stalled. Both machine and I were overheated.

In the kitchen I poured lemonade and took it to the front step and sat to sip and cool. Puppy lay stretched out on her side in a newly mowed section, snapping up only to bite at an itch. She acknowledged my "Hey, girl" by raising her head, squinting at me, and flopping her tail. Then she sank back down, sighed, and closed her eyes. Not even a boy on a bike who wheeled past called watchdog forth from her. *I know,* I told her, delighted that I could share feelings with a dog about the smell of grass and the warmth of sun.

From my center, I saw millions of blades of grass shouldering one another, a worm wriggling in overturned earth, desperate to rejoin the hundreds underground. A beetlelike insect crawled at my feet. *Bug, what is your name?*

I stopped absorbing the outdoors with my senses to pace off the moment. It had begun when I walked down the back steps and poured gas into the mower. I remembered feeling glad to begin an out-of-doors task instead of another indoor one, and glad, too, to move among living growing things instead of inanimate ones.

But I was experiencing more than that. In my inner self, God was interpreting life in his garden to me as I mowed. It was out from my union with him that I saw lawn lines, colors, and textures. *These worms, blades of grass weren't left by a Creator who tiptoed back to heaven. You're here . . . resident in me.*

Full of love for God and grass, I jumped up,

74

pulled the starter cord, and roared past the side of the house toward the backyard. As grass flew, Spirit communicated to spirit: "Live in moments."

I understood. *That is how life is meant to be lived—in a series of moments like this one and the others at the sink and clothesline—ones separated from all others, each with no afterward—each out of my union with God.* I wheeled down a hill and circled the base of the clothesline. *God and I united in a series of moments that stretched through the rest of my life. Doing this together . . . then this. . . .*

I ducked branches that hung low from the maple tree. *I haven't been chosen and sent out to live FOR Christ. I've been adopted by Father and allowed to live a moment at a time WITH him. My life was meant to be a succession of present-tense experiences in which I am occupied in him instead of preoccupied with myself.*

As I continued to mow the backyard, I reviewed the guidances that had led to this one and scattered gratitude before the power of the Highest. Then, with the mowing finished I brought the rake from the garage and began to comb the lawn and marvel to God that drivers didn't stop to stare at the phenomenon on the corner of Maple northeast. *The Holy Spirit guided me into truth here on the lawn and motorists on their way to the supermarket only glanced idly at me? The mailman only nodded "nice day" as he came down the path? Jehovah the Paraclete was communicating with flesh and traffic didn't back up to the burger drive-in?*

Outer man pulled the rake with long slow

strokes, but inner man wasn't constrained by the raking rhythm. That person was dancing in anticipation of the kind of life God was offering. Thoughts like children at recess burst from behind doors: "Do this moment's thing in God's presence . . ." one of them said. Another chimed in: "Then the next. . . ." Others danced and sang with them: "Walk in the Spirit . . . a step and a step. . . ." "Rest in God by moments. . . ."

With the last pile of grass dumped on the heap, I stomped my tennis shoes and went into the house. As I poured another glass of lemonade, I looked out of the window at the mowed grass and said silent wondering thank-you's to God for fellowship and tutoring over lawnmower and walked into the living room and into a new moment.

Because of the dirt on my jeans, I chose the wooden rocker instead of the upholstered green chair and eased down to enjoy good tiredness. *Doing nothing with you, Lord. Only resting and feeling the muscles you put in my body.*

I rocked in warm joy from the deep place within that was becoming more familiar. *Moments,* I thought out of that joy. For a while I only sat and rocked, knowing him. Then I began to think over what I was learning in a quiet, illuminated kind of reflectiveness—a process with which I was becoming increasingly familiar and one that I resumed during other quiet moments.

During those reflective times, I saw that the principle of living in moments had not been born over the mower. I'd known about it for years— known that it was the ideal way to live. I'd even

76

written about it myself: "Today is made up of
moments lived in the lap of God. Tomorrow
will be a moment multiplied."

Voices from paperbacked pulpits had been
urging me to live in moments since early in my
Christian life and had strengthened my resolve
to find a way. I'd stored their words in labeled
compartments inside my head and waited for Deity
to explain them to me so I could do them. I'd
expected exegesis with God as scribe that would
leave me crackling with power. But God was not
my scribe. He was my father. *First do this . . .
take your time . . . I'm here and will help. Now
do this. . . . See?*

Into summer as I reflected in the presence of
God, I reread others' words about living in union
with him moment by moment.

As I read, I nodded, smiling at the authors
because truth out there was becoming truth in
here. Andrew Murray was one who had loved
me through his book *Abide in Christ:*

*The thought of living moment by moment is of
such central importance—looking at the abiding
in Christ from our side—that we want once more
to speak of it. And to all who desire to learn the
blessed art of living only a moment at a time, we
want to say: The way to learn it is to exercise
yourself in living in the present moment.*

During the days before I discovered rest,
Andrew Murray's words had assured me that even
I could learn to live experientially in Christ. The
writer understood my infancy, wrote intimately with

a kind of loving concern that mirrored God's own. His words were warm with encouragement: abiding was something one did by moments. That made it sound attainable. *Surely, some day, Lord, you'll teach me how.*

Another whose stored words took on new meaning was A.B. Simpson. He had written in *Himself,* "I had to learn to take from Him my spiritual life every second; to breathe Himself in as I breathed, and breathe myself out. So moment by moment . . . we must receive."

I could remember the first time I'd read those lines. Jack and I had been parked in a secluded area by a stream one bright chilly noon. We'd just finished eating picnic sandwiches in the car and during the resting and digesting time afterward, I read *Himself.* The name of the town? The year? Gone. I remembered only the setting and the hope that had lodged within. *Lord. Please let that happen in me.*

But during the years since I'd read Simpson's lines, born-and-dying anxiety had kept pushing me to stockpile God's grace and power as though they were wartime scarcities. *So I'll have enough for always.*

Now, because I was learning to relax and lean, resting by faith in God the present One, I understood that his power and grace weren't commodities to hoard. They came out from him, and he was resident within me. "My child . . . let Me be in you the constant supply of all this, Myself," Simpson had written. God lived in me. That truth must become my faith/fact so that I could lean into him this moment, then the next,

onward into glory. "Breathe Himself in as I
breathed, and breathe myself out."

Hannah Whitall Smith had assured me, too,
that "we can only walk this path . . . moment
by moment. . . ." The lines I reread most often,
though, were the ones written by the Apostle
John. "Remain in Me . . . I am the Vine, you
are the branches" (John 15:4, 5, Berk).

Had Jesus been walking through a vineyard
with his apostles on the way to the Garden of
Gethsemane when he spoke those words? In my
mind I saw the eleven gathered close around him,
silent and sober as he talked and pointed to the
vines growing there.

My mind shifted to another vineyard. I was
seven or eight years old and living on my
grandparents' fruit farm. Summer mornings after
oatmeal, I closed the screen door behind me and
ambled down the dirt driveway past the big apple
tree under which the cider press sat, past the barn,
the spraying machine that I was never to touch,
on my way to the sandlot where I would set up
housekeeping. First, though, a side trip through
the grape arbors.

Babe, Grandpa's husky, sandwiched between
my legs, then ran between the arbors and finally
stopped under a low wire runner where he rocked
back and forth for a good back scratch. I walked
the rows peering at new leaves and tracing twisted
branches to a single vine-trunk, down, down the
wires.

Clusters of grapes still tiny and green hung
between the leaves. I looked without touching
because I knew that they were Grandpa's wages.

When they had ripened, I had permission to pick what I could eat, but now they were only for looking. In a few minutes, I would go on to the sandlot where I'd spend the morning playing big lady in a house I'd outlined on the ground with bricks. But stopping at the grape arbors was like stopping in church. They were the orchard at child level where I could study about winter into spring and summer, and branches and their vine, and ripening fruit.

I sorted through the memory with John fifteen open in front of me. Grandpa had been the vinedresser; there was fruit; dead branches piled to be burned. *You mustn't break off a branch or it will die,* Grandpa had said. Solemnly I had promised that I wouldn't. The branch had to stay joined to the vine because, inside where I couldn't see, life from the vine was traveling down, down through the branch so that finally we'd have baskets of grapes. Every moment while I stood there, that was happening.

I must remain united with you just that way, Lord. Moment by moment.

God *was* unfolding that Vine/branch life for me. But so often I hadn't believed that. He hadn't worked the way I'd supposed he would, according to a safe, predictable formula, so trust had come hard. I'd wanted God to recreate me in ways that fit my rationale. *God, creator of a rose? Of a star?*

Now, instead of waiting for moments of fellowship to "happen," I would try to initiate them myself. On a morning when Jack's parting kiss had been warmer than usual and the house was freshly vacuumed, I'd vow: "Today I'll do it. I'll live in moments". . . . and begin by straightening the kitchen in the presence of God. Before toast and crumbs were wiped from the counter, I was in dialogue with myself.

On days when the living room needed vacuuming but there was no time now and words for a manuscript eluded me, I walked carefully around the idea of moment living. Once fixed on Marion Duckworth things, my vision narrowed and moment living seemed a past tense ideal. Finally, (I'd be soaking in the tub or perhaps waiting in line) I'd experience a twinge like a spiritual pain, then a longing, and I'd vow to try again.

One afternoon I was doing something in the house and trying to rest in the presence of God but worrying that I'd fail the next moment. Then I thought, *Why not separate my life into a series of scenes? Like the book I am writing?*

My life *was* a series of scenes. Perhaps seeing it that way would implement moment living. God and I at the typewriter, in the optometrist's office. . . .

I would try.

Scene 1: Bedroom. Dog asleep on bed. Desk spread with papers, a dictionary, a Bible. *Action begins:* I enter, sink into God in my spirit, sit, and read a manuscript. I scribble a sentence, stare at the wall. Type a line; pace the room. Stop to scratch the dog and find my mind full of synonyms. I sink back into God again. Sit and pick up pencil. Leave to answer phone. Sit and pick up pencil. Leave to sign for package. Back at desk, I turn my mind back to God again, pushing through thick guilt. Action continues at desk until past noon when I get up to go make lunch.

Scene II: Kitchen. I bend in front of the
refrigerator to find the bologna for lunch and think
to God that we will eat together. Answer phone.
Dog barks insistently and I run to see why.
Remember that we're out of dog food and
write it on grocery list. What else was it? Soap.
I remember that I need to run a load of clothes. As
I load washer, I remember God and rest into him
but as I walk back to the refrigerator to find the
bologna, I feel disappointed and frustrated.

Until now I had no idea that each day was made
up of such action-packed scenes. Seeing that
helped me grasp that fact that my day wasn't a
sixteen-hour "succeed or fail for God" stretch.
It was made up of segments (I answer the phone,
I eat a bologna sandwich, I read the newspaper,
I open the mail). Each was a separate opportunity
to be and do in (or out of) union with God.

One thing I learned quickly. I was moving
around in my life at too fast a pace, more anxious
to get things done than to live out of my
relationship with God. If I were to live like a branch
in the Vine, fellowship and not accomplishment
had to become my priority.

But knowing that didn't help me do it. Those
days were full of vows and prayers and failures.
One part of me stood determinedly on the fact
that Jesus Christ's words "abide in me" were a
command and that the Holy Spirit was taking me
toward obedience. Another part of me counted
my failures and scorned.

I stood in the kitchen heavy with self-doubt
when I remembered Brother Lawrence. Ten years
or so before I'd read of that seventeenth-century

Carmelite brother assigned to the monastery kitchen, who practiced the presence of God there and who became known throughout Paris. I found the booklet, *His Letters and Conversations on the Practice of the Presence of God,* and read what he'd written to a nun: "I found no small trouble in this exercise, and yet I continued it, notwithstanding all the difficulties that I encountered, without troubling or disquieting myself when my mind had wandered involuntarily."

If Brother Lawrence could persevere in spite of his failures, so could I.

MOMENT
BY
MOMENT
(2)

8 Despite my determination to persevere, failure was still more common than success. Days without intimacy when I felt smothered by my outer reality slid by as though oiled slick. Then a moment after I finally did lean into the Holy Spirit and knew union again, I regretted: *Why have I waited so long?*

I glanced at the barren days behind and felt guilty. One time I pulled Brother Lawrence out of history and grabbed his hand *not worrying nor blaming myself.* . . . Another time he remained obscured by the centuries and I dug deep for a repentance that would relieve my guilt.

When a scene became so crowded with altars fashioned for confession that I could hardly move among them, I stopped still and pleaded for the assurance that Brother Lawrence was right. Was it or was it not sin when I failed to live in moments?

Through the Spirit of understanding, I began to see clearly again. In his writings, Brother Lawrence made it clear that this kind of fellowship was a way of life to be practiced, stumbling step after stumbling step. *Practice . . . do repeatedly in order to learn.* I was reminded of Andrew Murray's words in *Abide in Christ:*

The way to learn it is to exercise yourself in living in the present moment. . . . Each time your attention is free to occupy itself with the thought of Jesus . . . let your first thought be to say: Now at this moment, I do abide in Jesus. Use such time, not in vain regrets that you have not been abiding fully, or still more hurtful fears that you will not be able to abide, but just at once take the position the Father has given you: "I am in Christ; this is the place God has given me. I accept it; here I rest. . . ."

I shouldn't expect my mind to be unoccupied every moment. My way of life was very different from the monk in his monastery. Whenever I *was* free, I was to return to God and abide. And I was to build no altars for confession. *Rest.* Then do this moment in God's presence, loving and being loved, as though it were the *only* moment. Each time the habit would grow a little stronger. I would become a little more conscious of the truth that God lived in me.

Both the monk and the minister agreed that this was a habit to be learned. So long as I persevered in spite of my failures, so long as I leaned into God each time my attention was free, I was being obedient.

I was inept at this. God knew it and I knew it. He didn't blame me, so I mustn't blame myself. When describing the born-and-becoming process, the

86

Book used words like *"learn* of Me"; *"Grow* in
the grace and knowledge of our Lord"; *"Grow*
up in every way toward Him who is the Head"
(Matt. 11:29; 2 Pet. 3:18; Eph. 4:15, Berk).
"Learn" and "grow" were words with time stretched
between their letters. To hold to a wrong attitude,
to commit a wrong act *was* sin, but being a learner
was not.

To continually sorrow and berate myself for
my incompetence would be destructive, not
constructive. I had committed myself to live in
Jesus Christ. Whenever my mind was free, I would
rest in his presence without worrying or blaming
myself for the times I had not.

I remembered a morning years ago with my
sons in the strawberry field. Before school was out,
I had promised to work in the berry harvest with
them so they could earn money for school clothes.
Very early on a chill June morning, I sat between
the rows, scooting on my seat on the damp
ground, searching among the leaves for fruit.

"You find any?" a son called from his row.

I shook my head in disgust. *Why,* I thought,
*have they opened the field for picking when
the strawberries are still green?*

I scooted farther down the row, pulled aside the
wet leaves and caught my breath at a cluster of fat,
ripe berries. *Surely these are brighter red, more
redolent than those of any other spring.*

I picked them, careful to leave the caps on, and
placed them gently in the carrier, then pushed the
carrier ahead of me and scooted down the row.
The next plants had only blossoms and pip-sized,
green berries, but now I wasn't angry. I would find

87

more. And the tiny, green berries were a promise of fruit. *They just need more time.*

And I needed more time—to learn and practice what I learned, to fail and still trust for success, to be able to live out of Christ in me and I in him union, to produce Vine fruit.

On an afternoon after I finished writing for the day, I carried the vacuum into the living room and attached hose, wand, and brush. I ran the brush over the sofa cushions with my head full of my own schedule, but when I began on the rug I remembered intimacy.

A new scene: me in the living room vacuuming, doing one thing at a time in your presence, Father. A deep breath, and I rested into God in me. In him, I vacuumed in front of the sofa and thought about nothing except the clean place I was making and the warm joy of spiritual union.

Then a nudge at my brain from a photo lying on a table or a jacket on the back of a chair. *That boy of mine has been so distant lately. Why?*

Torn. I wanted to be obedient—to trust God for my son and do this work this moment out of intimacy with him. *But I must know how to reach my son—must find out what's wrong. He might. . . .* My even vacuuming motions belied the sweating in my soul because I didn't know how to mediate my two selves. *Rest and trust,* I told myself. But born-and-dying insisted. *I must think about this problem now. Figure it out now. What if? . . .*

In my spirit, I turned away from my own thoughts. *I trust you* and let my body and mind experience the rest of faith. God was silent, unaccusing, and then gently, he pressed knowledge into my spirit. "I am the answer."

I stood motionless, holding the roaring wand in my hand. Born-and-dying was still straining to push the problem into my conscious mind—to think it through and be rid of the worry while I worked—to make its own peace. But I chose to turn away and rest by faith in the present God. *You are the answer.*

In the Strong Place, I found healing. The sun shone through the orange drapes and I vacuumed by its brightness. But I was free of the worry only so long as I vacuumed in God's presence, doing that and nothing more, and trusting him as the answer to my distant son. When I turned away, unsettledness like clouds formed, threatening. Those times I imagined that son sitting silently across the room answering in monosyllables. Back of my head insisted: *Resting and trusting haven't changed the facts. The problem hasn't been solved.*

As I detached the hose and wand from the canister and carried them to the utility room, I answered from born-and-becoming. *God is the answer.* Puppy waggled back into the living room from a bedroom where she'd hidden from the vacuum's roar. I set the magazine rack close by Jack's chair and the tray tables in a corner and moved on into the day, trusting again.

Scene: I am sitting at the table sewing on a button and thinking *with the Lord now*. Back of the head worry pushes its way forward, severing rest. I commit the worry to God and live in the rest of faith. When my mind returns to worry again, I nod knowingly to God. *Learner . . . I am a learner.*

89

Scene: I am talking to Jack about the newly fallen snow. Worry presses at me and I turn to listen to it. From the Holy Spirit, a reminder to trust/rest for the worry and I turn back, grateful. Old self struggles for my mind; I do not panic now, only breathe trust to God and rest.

On another day after work, I brought a pot of tea into the living room, sank into the sofa, and breathed deeply of ease. Family was in the room, too, but occupied with their own early evening activities. In my niche on the sofa, I felt the security of relatedness, the privacy of individuality.

Had I thought, *A new scene with you, Lord,* and leaned into him? Or had born-and-dying seen the pause and pressured me with tomorrow already when a son came out of his room and sat beside me?

He turned toward me. "Mom, you know that guy I was telling you about? Well . . ." His words pushed one another to get out of his mouth; his face bore vulnerability like baby in the crib. He sat inches from me: fuzz on the lip, sideburns; a child/adult confiding in mother. This was a moment becoming more rare as sons grew up; a moment to listen in union with God and Holy Spirit.

In the back of my mind, born-and-dying pushed to gain access. *You can still plan tomorrow while he talks. Otherwise you'll fall behind.*

I gave my eyes to my son, but in my head I began to plan tomorrow.

From the other side of my within, I sensed the desire to abide. *Choose.* Inside, where no one could see, I chose and turned back to rest in God and listen to my son. With tomorrow given back

90

to God, the moment became one to be bronzed. Born-and-dying still pressed like a crowd at a barrier, but in the secret shelter of the Most High, I was safe.

In Spirit light after my son had gone again, I sat seeing this need of mine to keep careful control of my life. Before, "finish this and plan for that" had seemed to be efficiency polished to a high gloss, and I had been proud of it. Now I realized that it was keeping me from intimacy with God. *Rid yourself of the old nature . . . be renewed in your mental attitude . . . put on the new nature . . .* (Eph. 4:22-24, Berk).

Because of the Holy Spirit, I began to see other ways of thinking that were separating me from fellowship with God. One afternoon during this learning time, Jack and I stopped at a grocery store and while I consulted my list, he pushed the basket down aisles. We stopped to compare two pounds of spaghetti against four pounds, and this kind of toilet tissue against that, and then pushed to the rear of the store for milk from the dairy case and back to the front for lettuce from produce. "Done," I announced, and he pushed into a familiar clerk's line to wait.

When it was our turn, we loaded our items on the counter, and I squeezed past him to watch the clerk tally prices. As usual, Jack teased her about the sunshine she was missing and reminded her innocently that this was discount day so everything was half price.

He paid her in cash and she handed him bills in change. "Six, seven, eight, ten," she counted out. He handed the last bill back to her. "Give me ones

91

for this two-dollar bill, will you? I hate these things."

I moved away from the checkstand toward variety. Why couldn't he simply accept the new two-dollar bills? I wanted to keep walking—to separate myself from my marital half. Why did he have to be so persistently individualistic, even in little things like this?

Spirit light illumined my thoughts as I stood in front of a row of boxes of chocolate candy. I had been living this moment turned away from God. My husband had a right to object to a two-dollar bill if he wanted to. *I* was wrong. Had I been angered about it because I'd carried resentments from other scenes into this one? Perhaps because he hadn't fixed the rocking chair yet? Reluctantly, I saw that I had.

As Jack approached me pushing the basket of groceries, I turned to God and away from my born-and-dying self. *I'm sorry, Lord.*

I fell in step with my husband and pointed to a funny bunny card on the rack as we walked by. We waited while I chose a bottle at the perfume counter and sprayed myself with a sample. The door to the parking lot opened automatically and I walked through it face-to-face with God and loving Jack. I'd left the resentment in the aisle in front of the chocolates.

The memories of those moment experiences and the habits that interfered were piling up inside my head. In each, I had been able to isolate and identify a single born-and-dying way of thinking. *This is interrupting my fellowship with God.* I didn't need to run to the bedroom each time, fall

on my knees, and cry, "Wretched woman that I
am"—to dredge my soul for sincerity that would
convince God that I was sorry and alleviate my
own guilt. I simply needed to act the way I had in
the grocery store: see my sinful attitude, agree with
God about it within, and turn away from it and to
him again. When necessary, I'd have to apologize.
That *was* repentance.

I wasn't repenting for my sketchy ability to
practice God's presence. I was repenting of specific
wrong ways of thinking. Up ahead, there would be
more. Each time I recognized one, agreed with
God about it, and turned away to rest by faith in
his presence, I could go on to fellowship.

Part of me insisted that true repentance was
accompanied by weeping and sackcloth and that
if I were sincere, I wouldn't repeat the sin again.
But the Holy Spirit assured me that I was doing
scriptural truth; that behavioral changes came
slowly. I wasn't to concern myself with how many
times a day I had to turn away from born-and-
dying to God. As often as necessary, I was to
do so.

From my own experience in the grocery store,
I saw, too, that worry or resentment or any other
without-God way of thinking, need not splash from
one scene into another. When I turned away from
my without-God self, I was refusing those attitudes
mind-space, refusing to allow them to settle as
residents. *God* was resident. Whenever I leaned
into him again, I was renewing that fact and freeing
him to fill me with his attitudes that moment and
on into the next.

When a son stomped into the kitchen and told me the new thing he planned, I had a chance to live those principles again.

"No," I told him. "You may not do that."

"Well, it's not up to you to decide. It's up to me."

I stood firm on my decision and he stormed out. I wanted to shudder tears into the empty house, to pace the floor. But I turned away and to God in rest. *You are the answer. My son belongs to you. Keep him from the power of the evil one.*

PART THREE

LOVE

❧

9 I found that whenever I practiced the rest of faith, I was loving God back.

Loving him happened naturally during intimacy when my humanity settled and I thought/worked/played in his presence. I was face-to-face with God in my spirit, with my born-and-becoming, like-God nature united with his. Love was at my center, filling me within. I was living in the Person called Love. Nature mingled with nature. Love was *in* me, flowing out of me, back to him. In my spirit, I adored him without words out of joy deeper, richer, quieter than the human kind. I formed single, awed adorations: *Lord. God.*

Along the way I saw the Scripture of it. It is as John wrote: "We have come to know and have believed the love which God has for us. God is love . . . We love because He first loved us" (1 John 4:16, 19, Berk). I had come to know the love which God has for me, and with the love with which I was loved, I loved him back.

In Christian childhood, I didn't know how to love

God. At first conversion's flush when knowing was new, I felt awe for God like an ongoing gasp over sunrise as I bathed my babies and cleaned my apartment. I wanted to know more about undefined deity so I studied and prayed and worshiped and moved among other Christians. Awe grew as I learned that his power was greater than the combination of every historical human mind.

But love him? How did one love God? I wondered as I bought my sons thick pretzel sticks in the candy store near our New York City apartment early in my Christian life and later as I sat in the pews of the churches Jack pastored.

Was love for God a feeling that I could generate for him if I prayed with enough intensity? Or one that God would generate in me through a filling with the Holy Spirit some quiet night as I prayed and waited? Or did man-to-God love originate in a believer's intellect, arising out of what one knew to be true about him? Perhaps the essence of love for God was none of these. Perhaps it was simply unhesitating obedience: "If you love Me, keep My commandments" (John 14:15).

I tried to feel love out from myself as I prayed, but I could produce no emotion to match the word. About ten in the morning, with Mark on his stomach in his crib for a nap and family absorbed into their weekday places, I collected the Bible I studied from and settled on the sofa in the tiny parsonage living room.

Slowly, so that each word could soak into my brain and disappear, I read: "But God proves His own love for us by Christ's dying for us when we were still sinners" (Rom. 5:8). *Think,* I ordered myself. *Think of what the Son has done for you. Say grateful words back. Say, "I love you" to God.*

But I couldn't feel "I love you" the way I did for Jack, and I wouldn't mouth the words. *You're not grateful enough for Jesus' death on the cross,* I castigated myself. But still I did as I always had and prayed formal words of gratitude engraved in gold on parchment. "I am grateful, O God my Father, for your love for me. Were it not that you sent your Son to die for me. . . ."

After I had interceded for the list of requests I kept in a proper booklet printed especially for that purpose and put Bible and booklet carefully away for tomorrow about ten, I rose empty and guilty to do a good work as an offering to God.

Occasionally, I did feel *thank you, I love you* and mean it in my heart. But those were extraordinary times prompted by a communion service or a gift of blessing. Why couldn't I love God out from myself continually, the way I loved Jack, my sons? *Perhaps that kind of love can only be experienced human being to human being; perhaps it isn't possible man to God.*

But others seemed to love him that way. They stood in church services and said, "I love Jesus so much. . . ." These were people that I *knew. They do love Jesus,* my experience confirmed. I saw Love in the gentleness on their faces; heard him in the words they spoke, and in acts of kindness toward me and others.

I searched their faces and listened to what they said for clues to their secret. But the key to loving God was hidden somewhere deep in their spirits.

So I loved the only way I knew: service out of gratitude; obedience to the letter of the law. *Perhaps if I live obediently, God will fill me with the Holy Spirit of Love within.*

During Jack's years as a pastor, I had walked the Christian life with careful, precise steps and packed and unpacked dedication to serve God from one parsonage to the next and offered my walk and my work up to him. Daily I'd chided myself to walk circumspectly and do love with hours and sweat.

Jack chided me gently about religion out of duty. On a morning when Mark refused sleep and I postponed devotions until his afternoon nap, Jack breezed in from the church. "Ride with me. I have to pick up supplies for the church."

"But what about Mark? Anyway, I was planning to have devotions during his afternoon nap."

"Let him sleep in the car. And we can pray and share together as we drive."

Dutifully, I went. But guilt feelings rode between us and Jack realized it. He glanced at me as he drove down the hill to town and began talking from deep conviction. "God means for us to enjoy our relationship with him. . . ."

I'd heard it from him before. *Enjoy?* To enjoy my relationship with God, I'd have to have personal loving feelings toward him, wouldn't I? I had none. I had to *do* love. For me, there was no other way.

Deep in my spirit I still longed to love God with my whole heart, soul, mind, and strength. Marion the reborn kept searching the Scripture, kept pressing God for the way.

LOVE

Here on the other side of the years, I understood.
I hadn't been able to love God because I didn't
believe that he loved me. My old image of God as
one who saw a faceless world like the press of
New York City strangers at rush hour had been
wrong. He saw each face, heard the twisting of
each soul. He loved each of his created ones
individually, unreservedly, as fathers do.

Because God loved me individually, he wanted
to maintain a separate, intimate relationship with
me. God, not Marion Duckworth, had originated
and initiated the idea of he/me fellowship. Out
of his love he foreordained it, sacrificed for it,
revealed it, shared his longing for a more perfect
form of it. At new birth when he loved me to
himself, that union began. From that moment, we
were united, Spirit with spirit. But my old mind had
refused to believe in his love and hung back, not
daring to rest.

Now my mind was being renewed. I did know
and believe in his love, not only *for* me but *in* me,
filling my own spirit. Old habits and ideas weren't
preventing me from experiencing that union. When
I rested, I loved and because I loved, I trusted and
wanted to obey.

No more was obedience the act of walking heel
to toe along a straight biblical line. The desire to
obey came from deep within me now, where the
Spirit lived and was writing his laws upon my heart.
If I was living in fellowship with God as I mixed a
meat loaf in the kitchen or brushed Puppy on the
lawn, I sensed God's nature in my own spirit where
we were one. Those moments I longed for my

101

outer person to match the inner; for my human brain and face, talk, and movements to communicate his nature.

The morning the doorbell rang I was at my desk, eyes closed, head cupped in my hands, searching inside my head for words to make the paragraph I was writing lie gracefully on the paper. Puppy, who had been curled beside me in her bed, jumped startled from sleep as I did from my concentration.

It was someone I knew selling products door to door. I invited him in. After we sat, he produced a brochure from his pocket. "Have you ever used these?" The brochure described a line of household cleaners.

I sat back and smiled at him from the Spirit. "No. Tell me about them."

As I listened and asked questions, I measured the peace and joy within and marveled at their dimensions. From past experience I knew that before I learned to rest in Christ and live out of his nature in me, I would have invited this man in and been polite. But part of me would have raged at the interruption and length of his stay, and tried to hang on to the thread of thought I'd been tracing at my desk. The other part of me would have insisted on cordiality no matter how forced and would have chastised and left me shamed for hours.

Now, there was no such battle. I was resting in the presence of God and loved from him as I listened.

For years I'd prayed and waited and prayed again to be able to identify the sounds of God communicating to me so that I could know his will

and share his nature. Now, because of intimacy I
was able to hear him with the ears of regeneration.

Those early years I'd hoped that *today* a voice
would pierce my outer reality like God speaking
to Samuel in the tent: "Marion, Marion, Marion."
During private devotions, I'd prayed with my ear
straining the rural silence for a message more
distinctly personal than illuminated Scripture,
but heard only the sounds of the countryside.

After years of sermons and study had formed
Bible doctrine in me and I knew that to the
Christian, God isn't "out there," but "in here"—in
me—I prayed and listened for sounds from the
Spirit within. *Speak, Lord.* While I prayed for words
from God with one part of my mind, another part
still disbelieved that God the King would really
communicate continuingly with a face-in-the-crowd
believer like me. *Not the nature of the conversion
experience,* I reasoned.

I clung to the fact that God had spoken clearly
to me a half-dozen times or so in my life. Once
as I walked down a street, once as I lay in the
sun. Directives: "This is the way; walk ye in it,"
that sliced through the noise in my head. *More,
Lord. Today.*

But what did God's everyday voice to his
children sound like? To be obedient, I had to be
able to recognize and understand his guidances as
he applied scriptural principles to my life. How did
God sound to a Christian fisherman in Tiberias as
he sat mending his nets in the sun? To his wife as
she patted dough into cakes and tended their
growing family? We of the multitudes from first-
century Galilee to the twentieth-century international

community—how are we to hear him? Divinity's
thunder or the sound of many waters isn't for
noons at the lunch counter.

God's everyday voice had been described by
many as "still and small" like the one he used with
Elijah. Did that mean that he speaks to men during
their everyday in an audible voice—one with
frequency and modulation?

He *did* speak to men; accounts of his message
were recorded in the Bible. He *could* speak in any
way he chose, but it hadn't been in an audible
voice that he'd spoken to me when he'd issued
directives. They'd been biblically rooted thoughts
to my mind, from outside my own pattern of
thinking—ones so startling that I knew they
were from him.

Hannah Hurnard agreed with others that God's
everyday voice was "like the voice of conscience."
God thinks in us. Vainly, I had strained to
distinguish his thoughts from the rabble in
my head. To separate Thought from thoughts.
His? Mine?

As I strained for a communication from God
and a still small though did stand separate from
the others, I stared at it frowning, disbelieving its
authenticity. It was too closely mingled with other
thoughts, even though it did seem different in
origin. *Genuine or counterfeit?* I wavered. *How
can I be sure?* Fearfully, I edged away.

I knew that sometimes I stared suspiciously
at thoughts because I wanted to hold them at
arm's length. Hannah Hurnard understood why:
"Certainly that voice will often urge us to attempt
things that we do not want to do, or fear to do

104

because perhaps they look foolish. . . ."

It was because I didn't want to do something
that might make me look foolish that I turned away
from a peculiar inner urging one morning. I was
working at a job outside of our home then, and
now I had time off.

Since breakfast I'd been scrubbing, sorting,
polishing, and straightening, thinking in a narrow
circle as I washed the cookie jar (sons want
cookies), as I cleaned a shelf (need coffee and
vanilla). In the midst of the melange of Duckworth
trivia, thoughts of an acquaintance I hadn't seen
in months came to my mind like a stranger at the
door. That acquaintance was deeply troubled,
I knew, and had seemed alone in her struggle.

Call and invite her to lunch.

I stared dumbly at the phone. *I barely know her.
She'd think I was crazy. Why should she want to
come here to lunch?*

Silence within.

I turned away from the phone and opened the
refrigerator to rummage through the leftovers for
my own noon food.

Two weeks later she was dead. I cried and paced
in front of the phone, hating myself, wishing I
could believe the events were coincidences,
wondering whether the luncheon would have
made a difference, repenting, and sitting dulled
with horror.

Anxiety begged for clear, definite guidances.
(Shall I go back to work? Fly east to visit my
family?) Then I had no abiding sense of God's
presence in which to rest by faith, assuring me that
he would show me what to do. *I need to hear God*

tell me his will, I trembled before the stove, the washer. *Speak your will loudly, Lord, so I won't make mistakes.*

Now I didn't need God to shout guidances at me any longer. I knew that since God was Spirit, he communicated spiritually to his children in a nonverbal way called "fellowship," the language of the Person-Vine to the person-branch, not physically with ear sounds. Until now, though, I'd been so full of the sounds of my own soul that I'd been unable to sense his Spirit communicating to my own.

In the stillness of rest, I became sensitive to my Spirit/spirit nature where God abides and where he illuminates biblical truth. Because that nature is seedling of the Father with a character and attitudes like his, it is continually ready to do his will.

If the phone rings while I'm eating lunch and I rest in his presence as I say "hello," I will turn away from impatience because my soup is getting cold and listen sensitively to the friend who needs to tell me how it is.

But it isn't always easy to obey. In an instant I can turn away from Love and become my without-God self again. For the choices are often more costly than a cold bowl of soup.

But abiding in Jesus Christ is the best of all ways to live. I know that now. So finally I return to rest by faith, to love and be loved and to choose to obey because that is the way of love. If I am living in God's presence, I *can* choose his will, for it is already the desire of my reborn spirit. I want to please Father more than anything, so I get out of

106

LOVE

the chair to apologize or to go to my purse for the
money he wants me to give. Spirits rejoice, Father
and child, in a way I cannot separate.

But soon I look down the day to next time,
wishing for guarantees. *A next time like this time
and one after that.* I become unsettled, afraid of
the evil hiding in me that is quiet for now, but that
will pull at me later to disobey. I wish for it to be
gone so I can avoid the struggle, for obedience
to be second nature like brushing my teeth. Like
Marion of old I want to be able to generate
holiness out from myself, so I can be sure to win
for God every time. I do not want to have to fail
and persist until I win and my outer person is in
harmony with the inner.

In my renewed mind I am amused at myself.
*Are you that foolish, that you would now come
to perfection with the flesh after beginning with
the Spirit?* (Gal. 3:3, Berk) I ask myself.

You *are* that foolish, I tell my dark side. And
I turn my back and abide in God's love.

WILL

⁘

10 Into fall and winter and another spring as I rested and lived in Jesus Christ and failed to rest and lived in my self. I kept contemplating the separate lives in me—Marion old and Marion new. With each choosing they were becoming more clearly delineated.

One October afternoon, I raked leaves into a pile. *The mystery of seasons, Lord. The wisdom of trees to bud and leaf and shed since their genesis. . . .* As I mounded leaves, I planned love by phone to a depressed friend when I was finished. *I'll sweep the porch, and then make the call.*

But as I walked up the back step and saw the cracking wood, I thought, *This thing is still broken. And look how chipped the porch paint is! Why can't they clean up that mess next to the garbage can: empty oil cans, a rusty muffler, a tarp, a pail, and a rag from the last time they washed a car!* Old Marion grabbed the scene with her eyes and her brain and brooded over the image at the

phone and in the bathroom as she set her hair
in rollers.

Finally, again, I turned to God—away from life
and into Life. *Make me new,* I prayed in surrender,
and sensed my resurrected center. As my attitudes
changed again, I marveled at my own re-creation
in places I couldn't see.

Seasons moved into one another and I
fellowshiped and turned away. Each time I
fellowshiped, I became more familiar with the
dimensions of my natures, because the Holy Spirit
was illuminating my mind. Here was the old,
anxious over tomorrow. In that born-and-dying
state, I sat hunched tightly in my soul at the
kitchen table writing a "to do" list, shut in with the
knowledge of my own weakness and the outsized
life I had to live. This was my birthroom way of
thinking, stubbornly alienated from God, a soul
isolated, must cope/can't cope.

I leaned into God and trusted him for things to
do and rested in Peace solid beneath my center.
This is my new nature. . . . Before abiding, the old
had seemed to be all there was of me. Now I knew
the two and knew that I was an individual created
by God and given the power to choose between
old and new moment by moment. The times that
I chose to turn from isolation to God, through a
parting in my anxious soul I sensed my Spirit/spirit
center and knew again: *this is home. God in my
spirit is home.*

In the six-year-old part of my head, I had
vaguely supposed that my abiding relationship with
Jesus Christ began when I started to practice the
rest of faith moment by moment, but that wasn't

true. God had placed me in Jesus Christ when I
first believed, and at that moment he had begun
abiding in me.

Now I was learning to abide in him—to believe
and live in his presence, so that we could have
fellowship and I could receive from him moment
by moment whatever I needed for life and
godliness. It wasn't that I established our abiding
relationship when I began to rest in him. I once
had thought, *If I live in his presence and keep
him in my mind, I am rooted in the Vine; if I don't
I am not.* But God had established our union.
I was learning to actualize what was already true.

In my born-and-dying nature I live isolated from
God and independent; in born-and-becoming, I live
completely dependent on him. When Jesus spoke
the John fifteen words on crucifixion eve, he was
introducing the apostles to that kind of inner
dependence. No longer would they be able to go
to him with their questions, "Master, why? . . ."
No more sermons on a hillside, no parables along
the roads, or words to calm their storms. Now he
would indwell their spirits through the Comforter.
They must learn to depend upon him just as
completely through their spiritual union as they
had through their physical one.

I thumbed back to earliest years before I learned
to lean into God within. There seemed to be no
"me" then, only a Marion who was the sum of her
roles. That Marion had no sense of her own
separate personhood. Her true, God-created
spiritual self was imprisoned within a false,
unhealthy personality. Both "selves" were
intricately intertwined so that she was unable

111

to distinguish the one from the other.

I remembered the person I had been in one of the parsonages in which we lived. *When was it? What date on the drugstore calendar that marked our days then?* It ran into others in my memory, like a wash of watercolors. In each there were moments quick as a daydream.

The weather must have been bad because my young sons were playing on the floor in the living room. I seemed to remember blocks: red, green, and yellow, stacked precariously, and a son adding, "Just one more to make it higher." Matchbox trucks with Lincoln Logs to build a city around them. Toy box litter when the living room becomes the playground.

I had been stepping between trucks and children to kitchen, to bedroom, to kitchen, carrying clothes to put away or clean sheets for a bed.

"See this, Mom?" a son asked, and I knelt to praise a childish creation.

"Do this with me, Mom?" and I became playmate, stacking one more block without knocking the tower down. A rainy afternoon mother. *Busy, busy. Smile hard. Move fast. Friendly. Confidence that says, "Everything's OK."*

Somehow, then, I was in the bedroom, sitting on the edge of the bed, leaden with self, staring at the wall, tired from straining to confine the day's anxiety and guilt.

The door opened and I sprang up and into straightening or dusting. "Lookit, Mommy." A son had a car in his hand and was kneeling on the linoleum, moving its wheels furiously back and forth. "Lookit what it can do!"

112

I took the car in my hands, slid it on the floor,
and made warm mother sounds. When he left to
join his brothers, I dropped my arms at my sides,
closed my eyes. *God. God.* I wanted the efficacy
of the name to burst power over me and wash
away the ungodly with twin streams of peace and
joy that would continuously splash my soul.

The incident faded in my mind then, like the
ending of a dream and I remembered only hidden
heaviness.

I remembered that Marion in another parsonage,
on an afternoon, ironing Cub Scout uniforms and
praying that a Spirit breeze would fill her with
patience to cope with children who wouldn't play
outside and a clock that wouldn't stop ticking away
the hours.

"Don't play with Kitty underneath the ironing
board, Mark," I warned, struggling not to load the
words with my own stored-up feelings. I pressed
the iron harder into the cloth so that the metal
snaps popped down/up/down under the strokes.
*A new creature, Lord. Make me new the way
you promised. A creature full of yourself.*

Re-creation would come in a personal pentecost.
God the great and good would fill me and control
me. His presence would overwhelm me continually.
My personality would be transformed. No more
struggle to pull a balky ego down the narrow way
that leads to life. In an instant like the last day,
I would be full of God and emptied of me.

I sat in today putting the pieces of truth together.
God *had* made me new, but not by superimposing
his self on mine so that I lost my individuality.
Instead, when I cried, *Help me, I don't know who I*

am, and submitted to the circumstances that
followed, I developed an acceptable sense of
personhood; my reborn spiritual nature became
freed from the strictures of my unhealthy self. I
could choose to obey God, instead of choosing the
action that would salve my wounded ego. *I want to
do God's will. I choose to do God's will. I act to
do God's will because of the Strong Place.*

Since earliest mother-and-me days, old Marion
Duckworth had been choosing to do the things
that provided acceptance and love. When I was
in grade school, I wore my stockings to school
because mother, who was my authority, said
I should and I needed her love. But when I was
sixteen, I rolled my half socks down to my ankles
as soon as I was out of sight of our house. For
neither Grace nor Blanche nor any of the others
with whom they walked arm-in-arm were wearing
knee socks with mid-calf length dresses like mine,
and I needed the approval of my peers more than
that of my mother.

That approval failed to come, so I bowed lower,
searching for nods in remote corners of the
corridors during the week and in the bleachers
on Friday night. I chose to accept a pound of
humiliation for an ounce of acceptance.

Then Jack came and loved me wholeheartedly.
I dared do nothing to threaten that love. We were
married and lived in a downtown New York City
apartment. After work, we walked the dog and
then sank on the sofa, sitting close. We'd compare
"my day and your day" and talk about plans for
the evening.

"What's for dinner?"

I thought my way through the contents of the refrigerator and cabinet. "Tuna fish? Hash? Eggs?"

"Let's go out. Shall it be the Original Joe's for spaghetti or corned beef sandwiches on Forty-second Street?"

I'd search his face. Did he want spaghetti? Was it safe to say yes? On one level, we were playing a love game, standing close, whispering softly, "Whatever *you* want." But on a deeper level, I was cringing, not daring to make choices he wouldn't like for fear he might reject me.

When we were reborn in Jesus Christ and moved from a city apartment to a series of rural parsonages, I subordinated my personal preferences to those of our congregations in order to be acceptable to all. But I was becoming hungry to be a person with a will of her own. I wanted to want and then to do. To plant geraniums instead of the petunias on sale. To choose to lie on a blanket in the park and eat cold chicken instead of having it hot with gravy at the kitchen table.

I was becoming angry over my own passivity and shifting the responsibility for it to the shoulders of others. *Why don't they pull me off my knees— insist that I stand at eye level, speak my mind?*

Part of me was adamant. *God means for you to subordinate your will to that of others. . . . "In honor preferring one another,"* the Bible says (Rom. 12:10, KJV). If I exercised my own will, wouldn't that be the mark of self-centeredness? Wasn't submission the mark of a saint?

I kept the image of Jesus Christ bowed low

in the Garden of Gethsemane projected on my mind. I wanted to be as submissive to the Father as Jesus was. To be without a will of my own. For God to move in with the omnipotence of deity and crush my will. *Make your will so strong in me that I won't have to make choices myself. Take over. Decide. Then fill me with the power to do. Move in and create a new me.*

God didn't answer. So I bowed lower and pushed harder, stiffening myself against the Marion person begging to emerge. I prayed, "'Work in me to will and to do of your good pleasure' (see Phil. 2:13, KJV). Get me out of the way so that you can will and do instead of me."

Finally, I could exist will-less—in subjection to the whole human race—no longer. *I must have individuality* pushed as persistingly into my conscious mind as a seed through the hard earth. God's "I love you" was my spiritual spring.

I knew now that God didn't mean for me to live without a will of my own. He had created me to be a separate person—an individual with a personality of my own, with the ability to make my own choices. But from first breath, that volitional ability had been controlled by my without-God self.

At new birth my will had been regenerated— severed from the control of my birthroom nature. At that moment I could choose to obey God and depend on the Holy Spirit to energize me. But still I was making decisions out of a wounded ego.

I had to retrain my will. The Helper, whom the Father sent to represent Jesus Christ, would teach and strengthen me.

More and more frequently, I began to tell Jack
things that I'd like to do.

"If the weather's nice on Saturday, let's take
a trip east and hike into the woods."

"Let's go to Baskin Robbins for an ice-cream
cone for dessert. A dip of pistachio almond would
sure taste good."

"Let's take Puppy to the park/take a walk in the
snow/sit on the sofa and listen to records."

Jack was delighted over my new enthusiasm for
pistachio almond and walks in the woods. He *loved*
me; it made him happy to do things that pleased me.

"I'd sure like to be able to identify the birds we
have around here," I told him one spring day.
"Let's buy a feeder and hang it in the maple tree
outside the window."

Plastic feeders were on sale in a local store and
so were big bags of bird seed. Jack wired the
feeder to a tree limb that day, filled it with seed,
climbed down the ladder, and stood beside me.
"There," he said with mock exasperation. "I hope
you're satisfied. You've got your feeder."

Next time I was in the library, I found a book on
birds of the Northwest, brought it home, and kept
it on a table near the kitchen window. "Come
quick," he called from the window soon after.
"See? The tiny yellow bird near the top of the
tree? What kind is it?"

Another time he called me and pointed to the
tiniest, bubble-bellied flock high in the tree. "Do
you know their names?"

I called him when I spotted a different kind.
"Look quick. On the feeder. See? Black on their

117

chests like a bib. I'm going to look and see what
that one is."

As we sat at the table eating our own breakfasts,
we watched Mr. and Mrs. Sparrow eating theirs,
and the blue jays that swooped, tried to bully, but
couldn't perch on the narrow stand. The feeder
swayed in high winds. "But look at them hang on!"
we marveled. And "just like people" as they fought
for a spot.

With every expression of my individuality, I felt
Marion Siegel Duckworth forming in me. *This is
who I am: a person who likes butter brickle and
pistachio almond . . . who wants to know out-of-
doors things . . . who likes to listen to silence.* My
bones seemed to be thicker; my features more
clearly defined.

Every time I chose to eat later instead of now
or to go tomorrow instead of today, I was gaining
experience in choosing. The ground seemed to be
firmer under my feet as I stepped into morning.
But bird feeders and hikes in the woods were
only elementary choices—ones that expressed
my human personality and firmed it up for me.
Deeper within, I knew that I would have to begin
making harder choices. I shrank down into the
safety of Christian childhood again and showed
God my drooping hands and shaky knees. He
remained quietly firm and assured me of
his strength.

Then came Sunday terror when I lay across
the bed sobbing *I . . . can't . . . go . . . on . . .*
and sensed words firm with Divinity's authority:
"You must go on. You can choose to go on."

From the moment I put my feet on the floor on

my way to make a chocolate cake, I knew that it was my responsibility to choose to do God's will no matter how hard it seemed. Over and over I would have to decide whether I was going to give in to old self or obey and trust the strength of the Holy Spirit. God would work in me to restore a healthy sense of personhood; he would give me the desire to obey, provide guidances to show me how, and provide people to help me; he would provide strength within so I could persevere. But only I could choose.

Each time I obeyed, I knew more surely that I had believed correctly. God *had* asked me to choose to go on in spite of the way I felt. And because I had a free, independent will and a healthy sense of self now, and because I could live facing God and receive his strength, I *could* choose.

As the sounds of my soul grew more quiet and I could hear intuitively with my reborn spirit, I realized that on any day choices came head to toe. Would I brood because one of the family snapped instead of smiled or pray, *"Help them"* and go on? Would I admit to Jack that *he* was right or keep silent? Listen objectively to the one who was talking or let his words run off my mind while I gathered objections? Stop to pet Puppy and thank God for created things or rush into my next moment pricked with anger from the last? The choices were mine.

Truth pressed into my spirit and I saw now that I could have prayed to become will-less until my skin became parchment and God wouldn't have answered. I had been created to have a will of my own. "The Lord God charged the man: You may

119

eat freely from every tree in the garden; but do not eat from the tree of knowing good and evil" (Gen. 2:16, 17, Berk). *Choose. You must choose.* "If any man will to do his [God's] will . . ." (John 7:17, KJV). That from the Book.

A book, A.W. Tozer's *That Incredible Christian,* enlarged the truth for me. "It is inherent in the nature of man that his will must be free." For he is "made in the image of God who is completely free. . . . To remain a man he must make his own moral choices."

I'd misunderstood Gethsemane. Jesus Christ did have a will of his own when he prayed, "Father, if it be possible, let this cup pass from me" (Matt. 26:39, Berk). His human nature struggled to escape the cross; his divine nature understood the higher purpose. Face-to-face with the Father he surrendered and in intimacy rose, strengthened, able to die.

I'd misunderstood the meaning of submission. God "never wills or acts in place of man. He merely endeavors to bring man to the position of being disposed to will and to do his excellent will" (Watchman Nee, *The Spiritual Man).*

God had never intended me to wait passively for him to descend from heaven or ascend from within and control my will. He intended that my will be free—not controlled by born-and-dying or manipulated by him. Even though he lived in me, still he allowed me independent personhood. Would I choose to live in his presence, to listen with my spiritual ears, trust in his strength in me and obey?

Only when my personhood was secure—when

I no longer had to submit to others in order to
gain their acceptance was I ready to learn biblical
submission and humility. Real lowliness of mind,
that habit of esteeming others higher than myself,
isn't a human-being quality. It comes out from God
and is available to me only when I live face-to-face
with him. Then my inner person is bowed low.
When I live that way—as a branch in the Vine, love
for others flows from him through me, and I want
to step down as Jesus Christ did.

At every turn in the day, however, my self
stands stiff and unyielding. *Unfair. I deserve. . . .*
Later that day or on another long separated from
it, I submit and in Love esteem a brother higher
than myself. Something in me dies. When the
pain has stopped, I realize that it is pride, and
I do not mourn.

PRAYER
(1)

⁙

11 The clock radio clicked on to
KXL 750. Sound came hard on
my ears, setting time and place.
"The Governor announced new
budget cuts for state offices. . . .
Last night, the Portland Trailblazers
faced the Los Angeles Lakers
without Bill Walton. . . ." I lay still between the
sheets feeling around for the shape of my own day.

Things to do pushed from the back of my head
to the front. The weight of them forced my eyes
open, my feet over the side of the bed to the floor,
and down the path called morning. *Cans out for
recycling truck. Chicken from freezer. Breakfast.
Devotions.*

Devotions. A red item on my "to do" list, with
the clock as proctor without, and my born-and-
dying nature proctor within.

I'd begin by pulling the chair up to my desk.
With the Bible open in front of me, I'd dig around
the words of a passage, trying to uproot them and
plant them whole in my mind. "I will exalt Thee,

my God and King" (Psa. 145:1, Berk). *I must exalt God.* I tried to imagine myself pushing God up high through my deeds and attitudes like a king on a portable throne.

Then prayer. I'd open my card file and withdraw several from different categories: family, friends, the sick, missionaries, nation. A few opening words of reverence like a perfunctory morning kiss. Then *God speak to . . . God heal . . . God provide . . . God protect.* I must say the right words with the right amount of intensity. In the blackness of eyes closed, I sorted through piles of prayer words for a new way to verbalize my requests and fought shame for wishing the time were over.

I'd been learning to practice the presence of God through faith/rest during the secular part of my day. But in my inner mind I still saw devotions as the sacred half hour, separated from the rest as an altar from a lunch counter. I frowned at my own double-mindedness and looked to God questioningly for a way to make my private worship new.

One morning after the last bite of toast, I pushed away from the kitchen table and without putting away the orange juice container and wiping crumbs from the placemat, went directly into the bedroom and sank into God. Born-and-dying urged me up, to the hard chair at the hard desk, to the bold black letters and stiff prayer cards, to the prayer closet that I must fill with the sounds of reverence.

Rest, I reminded myself. *Sit here on the bed and rest in the presence of God.*

New me, the learner, obeyed. I breathed deeply

and relaxed. *I am in your presence, Lord.* For several minutes, I sat, hushed as midnight, eyes closed, mind forming no words, in intimacy with God in my spirit. Then I moved to the desk to read and pray.

The next morning and the ones after that, my without-God nature pushed harder for me to go right to the desk, to the card file, to the requests. But deep within I knew that the principle of rest belonged here in my prayer place—that my Tutor was urging me to choose to relax my body, rest my soul, and commune in spirit with him. He wanted to renew my attitude toward private worship.

Mornings as I served scrambled eggs to family in the kitchen, I began to look forward to rest in the bedroom in the presence of God. Sitting quietly at the head of prayer time was different from anything I had ever done before. *Risky,* old self warned. *You need that time to recite names and needs. Every one every day. To get it done and get it right before time to go to work.*

But born-and-becoming knew better. The truth seemed so obvious now: God meant for me to rest in his presence during my devotional time and to commune in Spirit/spirit intimacy, for that was the nature of worship. Words by Hannah Hurnard that I'd read and stored years before, I remembered now. Morning worship was a time to "Meet the Lord and listen to him" *(The Hearing Heart).* For her, devotions were a time of uninterrupted intimacy with the Lord of Love. By faith I believed that it would become that for me, too.

Minutes seated on the bed resting, thinking *you are here, Lord. I believe,* lengthened. I began to

want to worship God. In my spirit, I sang words
that came to me: "I worship and adore you,
bowing down before you. . . ." Then, I sat loving
him from my center.

When I was ready, I moved to the hard desk
chair and sat at rest in the presence of God, to
worship. Later instead of resting on the bed first,
I sat directly in the chair and began to worship
in my spirit. Some mornings, I said a hymn of faith
silently to him and the Kingdom within rang with
its melody. "A mighty fortress is our God." I
thought about the words and made them my own
declaration of faith. *My mighty fortress.*

Other mornings I sat to commune with God, to
worship, but I could sing no hymn, form no praise,
because my without-God self had begun picking at
someone's angry words, some care, the day before
and had grown fat and filled me within. Those days
I read quickly, prayed by rote, and left hungry.

One of those mornings, I looked for a psalmist
to put words in my mouth and read what David
wrote. "As a deer pants for water brooks so my
soul longs for Thee, O God. My soul thirsts for
God, for the living God. . . . My tears have been
my food day and night. . . . Why are you bowed
down, O my soul: why so restless within me?"
(Psa. 42:1, 2a, 3a, 5, Berk).

I began to pray David's words: *oh, God, see me
cast down and disquieted . . .* and then my own:
*and I know why. Yesterday, I chose to feel sorry
for myself. I refused to forgive. I'm sorry, Lord.
I repent.*

I was forgiven. Words of a chorus came from my

spirit because of intimacy restored and I sang them silently. "God is so good. . . ."

Often after that when I felt pushed to hurry or pulled inside my own head by feelings of uneasiness, when my soul seemed to have caved in and heaped rubble on my spirit and I knew God by faith and memory only, did I put Scripture's words in my mouth and speak them to him. One morning I would choose words that said how I felt. Another morning, I sat quietly before God until I could open my soul wide and let him look inside. When he had seen it all, I'd form some words. Perhaps first I would only say his name. *God . . . oh, God. . . .* Then some Scripture to stand on: "The Lord is the strength of my life; of whom shall I be afraid?" (Psa. 27:1, KJV). Or I prayed praise from David or Isaiah, John or Paul, giving the words time to sink deep into my spirit where God was waiting to make them live.

I soon realized that if private worship were to become a time when I communed Spirit/spirit with God, I would have to begin wherever I was. Was my soul cast down and disquieted? I had to tell God so. Was I worried? I had to let my anxiety spill out to him. I could use Scripture words or my own. But if I wanted intimacy more than any other thing, I had to let my outer vestments fall away and stand stripped to the soul so that I could know and be known.

Mornings after I had done that, I turned to the place in my Bible that I'd planned to study that day. Usually it was no more than a few sentences or a paragraph. Some mornings old self persisted in interrupting fellowship by parading her anxieties through my mind. I cautioned myself not to argue, but to turn quietly away and rest in the Vine. *You have seen my soul. You know my needs. I rest in your love.*

I used a variety of ways to study, but I knew now that the method was subordinate to the purpose. Devotional Bible study was a time to sit in the presence of God and be taught from the Scriptures by him. I knew that I must begin study by asking for his help, but instead of choosing words for the prayer from my proper pile, I looked to God in continuing intimacy and trusted him for illumination.

Slowly I looked at the verses with my eyes and let them seep into my mind. Some mornings I looked for the key verse or phrase in a passage and tried to determine exactly what the writer was saying. "We are writing to you about the Word of Life; He was from the beginning, we have heard Him, we have seen Him with our eyes, we have looked at Him, and our hands have touched Him" (1 John 1:1, Berk). "The Word of Life" was the key, I decided.

I read the verse from another translation and in my mind, said the passage in my own words. *John is writing this letter to me about Jesus, God's message of life. He is eternal. The apostles actually heard him speak, lived with him, saw him every day, even put their hands on his body.*

I thought some more. *These words are to me. The one who expressed the very nature of God Almighty—the Spirit of Christ—lives in me. John was excited because he had been living in intimate*

128

association with the Son of God. Here I am, living in intimacy with you, too, Lord. John and I are in awe. He saw you with his eyes, touched you with his hands. I see you in my spirit. In the Kingdom of God, I was bowed low before the throne in adoration.

I was still using my mind to explore the verses, reading other translations, using an English dictionary, a Bible dictionary, word studies, and other books on my shelves for reference as I always had. I asked myself questions and looked for answers. I tried to be sure I understood exactly what the biblical writer was saying with his words and how they fitted into the context. But now I was aware that each step was energized by the Holy Spirit ("See?" he seemed to be saying) because I was at rest and listening with my spiritual ears. I wasn't trying to dig truth from the Scripture and plant it whole in my life myself, to please God. I was letting him teach me. So long as I trusted, he would enable me to do it. Through that kind of study, my spirit grew stronger.

Whenever I was conscious of the presence of God as I studied the Bible, the concepts that I discovered led me to pray. "Beloved—divinely loved ones. . . ." *That makes me feel so humble, especially today because I know that you want me to show your patience and I've been dragging my feet.*

Or I'd find myself thanking God. "I praise Thee because I have been fearfully and wonderfully made . . ." (Psa. 139:14, Berk). *These fingers, Father. The organs functioning inside my body.*

*So many good things. My family, Lord. Thank
you for them. For Mark. I pray for him. Guide
him.* I was interceding.

I was beginning to understand something of
what "prayer in the Holy Spirit" meant. As I rested
in the presence of God, his Spirit filled mine and
guided my thoughts and words back to him.
Before I'd learned to rest by faith in his presence,
I often talked to God as though I were still isolated
from him, even though I was reborn. Now that I
was learning to live in the Spirit's presence and
strength, I found that I could pray out of that
Spirit/spirit union.

Intercession had been the hardest kind of prayer
for me. Whether or not a request for husband or
sons had efficacy depended on the sincerity and
intensity with which I said the words. If I was
worried about Mark when I prayed, I felt satisfied
that the force of mother love had pushed my
words to God. But I had to stiffen my will to pray
day after day for a friend I hadn't seen in years,
whose face I could hardly recall. But intercessory
prayer was a Christian obligation that no disciple
shirked.

Now I knew that my intercessory prayers were
being energized by the Holy Spirit. He knew and
loved each of these for whom I was praying;
I didn't have to try to manufacture feelings of
concern for them. Love was there in him and he
was in me. I still kept my card file current with
names and requests and read through them
occasionally to refresh my memory. With the
names and requests in my mind, I'd lean into
God and pray out from Spirit/spirit intimacy.

Born-and-dying still refused to believe that this kind of praying was acceptable to God. She was a Pharisee's child. *Follow the rules. Say the words exactly right.* She threatened tragedy if I disobeyed. But I knew her now. She was of the son who was born in the usual way who persecuted the one who was born of God's Spirit. I turned away and to God. "We are not the children of a slave woman but of a free woman" (Gal. 4:31, TEV).

In the presence of the Holy Spirit, I found that I could intercede without forming my thoughts into words, as though we had a way of communicating without alphabet language. I had prayed for Carroll and his family with words often. Sometimes, though, I prayed by thinking to God about that family in the parsonage of their country church. In union with God, I loved Carroll, his wife, their daughter Kathy, son Lee, and the others, and trusted in his fatherhood for answers to the requests that their names represented to me.

Because I was learning to pray in the Spirit, the words I used were ones that came out of intimacy with him and not paste-ups of yesterday and the day before. With these words I found that I could ask and intercede, praise, give thanks, and worship with freshness every day.

When my time of private worship was nearly over, I'd sit quietly stilled in my spirit. These past minutes I had been living in the place of the Spirit. I was ready to move into this piece of time called a day established in him.

PRAYER
(2)

❦

12 After morning worship I slid my
Bible into its place on my desk
and rose to put in a load of
laundry, take the dog out, and
put yesterday's newspapers away.
As I carried the hamper to the
utility room and began dropping
clothes into piles of wash and wear and regular
cycles thinking soap and bleach with my mind, my
spirit was water running over stones. I filled the
machine, clicked it on, and whistled "Let's go"
to Puppy. At the front door I "arfed" at her from
praise spilled over and chased her across the rug,
leash in hand.

I'd just come from the Kingdom where I'd been
listening with other ears, seeing with other eyes.
And though private worship was over, no postlude
had sounded. In my spirit I was still in the
sanctuary, praising.

Later, I sat at the desk that had been my prayer
closet, ready to begin the day's writing. A robin
stood still on the lawn outside my window with a

133

worm dangling from its beak. Through those other eyes I saw its red breast, its mouthful of breakfast. Without words, I bowed in my spirit before the Creator of robins and worshiped.

The robin flew off out of sight and I stared at the moment just past. When I told God my awe of him without putting it into words, had I been praying? I reviewed other moments when I'd shared an attitude of faith as I filled the washing machine or walked the dog. Those times I thought of as fellowship, but were they a form of prayer too?

What *was* prayer? Was it only the formal, verbal conversation "Dear God, bless Jack . . ." that I had with God?

That wasn't true, I knew. Prayer was spiritual communion. It was the sharing of selves.

I remembered a breakfast with Jack at McDonald's early one Sunday morning. While he went to order, I sat staring out at the October trees. Red and yellow leaves drifted to the ground and settled into a pile of autumn on the sidewalk. Awed at universal order, at beauty out of the window of a fast-food restaurant, I worshiped God without telling him why. He knew.

That had been prayer. *Set* times of prayer were not different from other times, Brother Lawrence had said. Now I understood what he meant.

Prayer and fellowship were inseparable, for prayer is the language of intimacy with God. When I lived in his presence and related the thing in hand to him moment by moment, whether I formed words *God help me* in my mind or simply leaned into him in surrender and unspoken dependence, I was communicating to him just as I had during

134

private worship. If one of the family came home
angry and in my spirit I gave him to God, that was
a prayer of intercession. Later, if I watered the
garden and saw tiny green beans, slivers hanging
on the vine where blossoms had been days before
and breathed wonder to the Creator of vines, that
was a prayer of praise.

One morning, while I was pondering prayer as
communion, I took out the manuscript I had been
working on from a file on my desk and began to
reread yesterday's work. At the second paragraph
a son burst into the room and held up an unironed
pair of pants. "I don't get the crease right when I
iron them. Would you do it?"

I hovered between born-and-dying anger over
the interruption by this grown-up child and born-
and-becoming's gentle, patient "No, I can't now/
yes, in a few minutes." Without putting the
thought together into a stack of words, I breathed,
You, God. I choose you. "Put up the ironing
board, fill the steam iron, and I'll be there,"
I had prayed.

Back at the desk, I read a sentence and stared
into the air for a better word. From their places
I pulled a dictionary, a thesaurus. The list of
synonyms bred in my mind and finally produced
an offspring that seemed just right. I wrote it down
and tried to decide how to finish the sentence
when I remembered a quote that might fit, but
I couldn't find it. I became angry at myself for
having a poor filing system. The anger grew and
became discontent because I had only a corner
of the bedroom to work in and not an office.

The peace of faith/rest was gone. I felt unkempt.

Finally I chose to turn away from anger-become-discontent and turned to God. The moment of my turning away was my prayer of repentance; the turning to God, my prayer for help.

Chin in hand, I sat putting a sentence together when I glimpsed a jotting on my note pad. "Visit in nursing home." How would I make time today? I breathed deeply and that breath became a thought to God: *Help me write this page* and I rested by faith.

The day grew older and every new hour was heavier than the last. During one, I struggled with the pieces of an article due shortly that I couldn't fit together. During the next, the mailman brought a letter built of tightly written innuendo. The washer drained on the floor. Workmen were tearing up the sidewalk outside our front door and Puppy wouldn't stop barking. With a wordless expression of trust, I turned away and to God for the article and the letter, the washer, and the sidewalk noise.

When I rested in the Holy Spirit, the day fell into perspective again. The letter I put in a file to wait its turn; the washer in a slot in my head marked *Jack.* I brought Puppy's bed from the living room and set it next to the desk where I could pat her quiet while I worked.

While I scratched Pup's ear and shushed her growls at the strange street sounds, I thought about the moment before when I'd spoken to God from my spirit and then about the other moments like it that day. Was that what Paul meant when he wrote "Pray without ceasing" (1 Thess. 5:17, KJV)? If I communed with God about the things that

were happening during the day, was I acting on
that Scripture?

I opened my Bibles for clues. "Pray
perseveringly," the Amplified New Testament read.
"Pray at all times," the Today's English Version was
translated. "Never stop praying," Phillips put it.

I'd pondered that phrase in parsonages while
Mark took his morning nap, trying to imagine
myself saying the properly put-together paragraphs
that I called "prayer" one after the other to God,
and knew that was impossible. "Pray without
ceasing" had been another of the mysteries of
the Bible.

Now I went to the living room and looked
through titles in the bookcase for a scholarly
interpretation and found Charles Caldwell Ryrie's
yellowed colportage book, *First and Second
Thessalonians,* that Jack and I bought when
it was thirty-five cents.

. . . Without ceasing . . . *is used of a hacking
cough. . . . Just as a person with a hacking
cough is not always audibly coughing though
the tendency to cough is always there, so the
Christian who prays without ceasing is not always
praying audibly and yet prayer is always the
attitude of his heart and life.*

Farther down the shelf I found Matthew Henry's
comments on prayer without ceasing in *The Quest
for Communion With God.* "Even when we are not
making actual addresses to God, we must have
habitual inclinations toward him. . . ."

. . . *The attitude of my heart . . . habitual*

137

inclinations toward him. When I lived face-to-face with God in me, prayer *was* the attitude of my heart, not just a proper Christian exercise—a "should" or "ought" or an expression of desperation at junctures during the day. I wanted to tell God my life: *See that robin; help me with anxiety*—to commune with him in my inner person at the same time that I communicated with the world with my outer person.

Until I had learned to sense the spiritual dimension within me, I couldn't have imagined the length, breadth, depth, and height that prayer could assume. This kind of prayer communion could be an ongoing dialogue during every day, the way Jack and I would touch minds from across the room with a look. *I love you. . . . I need help.*

But Jack and I didn't always communicate in intimacy, he from his chair, me from my snug sack on the sofa. Some evenings I avoided his eyes, kept hard to the page because my mind was stumbling over anger toward him or was preoccupied with Marion things.

And I couldn't communicate continuously with God, either, I told myself.

With a sagacity born of experience, I spoke back as parent to my own child. *Rest. Wait for Father to teach you more. Walk in the Spirit, a step at a time.*

Reluctantly, I went back to work hunting for action verbs to go with concrete nouns. After paragraphs, my mind began to edge away like a recalcitrant child to worry again over the letter (how will I answer it?) and the washer (will Jack be able to fix it or will we have to call a repairman?).

Mindquakes like these were splitting my hours

138

into fragments. I turned away from one problem
and turned to God to take care of it, but the
worry-rumble from that one seemed to set
another in motion.

The days ahead introduced new reasons
to worry:

A son who was away on a trip didn't call as
he promised.

The debit column of our budget weighed
pounds heavier than the credit.

The car was whining again.

Age sixty-five was only a dozen years away
and we had no retirement.

Self-to-self dialogue, I would think, and
remonstrate myself to fellowship.

*Perhaps these are unusually black days.
Perhaps when they pass. . . .*

In the Light I knew that wasn't true. To become
uneasy and live in that back-of-my-head brooding
place had been second nature since the days when
the relief check was late and mother's little black
change purse was empty. More than any other
mental habit, worry was still the one that was
keeping me from learning to commune more
continually with God.

Another workday morning, I sat down at my
desk to read a just-published article of mine,
paragraph by paragraph. I compared it to my
original manuscript, noting editor's changes. About
halfway through, when I came to a Bible passage
I'd quoted, I sat up, startled.

*Entertain no worry, but under all circumstances
let your petitions be made known before God*

139

by prayer and pleading along with thanksgiving.
So will the peace of God, that surpasses all
understanding, keep guard over your hearts and
your thoughts in Christ Jesus (Phil. 4:6, 7, Berk).

I read the verse again, not proofreading now,
but seeing it as if for the first time. Moments
before I'd read those words, part of my mind
had been forming worries around visual images
it was receiving.

"Look at that pile of papers. When am I going to
have time to get to them?"

"The dust and pencil shavings on the desk . . .
the bulging folder of mail. . . ."

"That dog hair and dust in the strip of sun on
the floor. . . ."

Each time, I was tempted to slump and stare off.
"When *will* I ever get caught up? I can't stand this
mess. . . ." and let my mind slide into the shadows
to worry over other, bigger problems.

From the words in the article in front of me, the
Holy Spirit shined out new truth: "Entertain no
worry. . . ." "Do not invite worry in like company:
Make yourself at home."

After my writing for the day was done, I brought
out *Word Studies From the Greek New Testament*
and settled in my favorite spot on the sofa with my
shoes off and a cup of tea on the table before me.

". . . We have here a prohibition which forbids
the continuance of an action already habitually
going on," I read. "The Philippian saints were
habitually worrying. Paul exhorts them to stop it.
The word 'nothing' is literally 'not even one thing.'"

I let his words settle in my head and then read

the Scripture again. ". . . Under all circumstances
let your petitions be made known before God."
Paul was strongly urging me to form a new habit,
not by haphazardly abiding: *Now I pray it, now I
don't,* but by telling God my needs consistently.

I stared out of the window at the plum tree, the
lawn, the street that ran past our house—symbols
of the real time/space life of which I was a part.
"Can I do it? When the mailman walks across the
street and to the door with too many bills? When
family slams in and out of the door with a string
of needs that have to be taken care of *now* and
old mind insists that I can never be adequate?

"Can I learn to tell God each worry—expose it
by saying it in clear, decisive language so that his
light can shine on it and change the way I think
about it? Under all circumstances? At the
clothesline, the desk, the shopping center,
the bank?"

One more time I wanted a sweeping guarantee
of success. To be able to stand tall before God.
"All that thou sayest I will do."

But Light cautioned. "Whoever lives in me and I
in him shall produce a large crop of fruit. For apart
from me you can't do a thing" (John 15:5, TLB).

On shaky knees, I began to try to do as God
was teaching me. "By faith, Lord. Because you
say so."

I heard God the Holy Spirit issue a warning and
found that I'd been thinking, *I'm afraid that my
son is making a wrong decision,* while I peeled
potatoes and turned hamburger into patties. I
spoke it in prayer. That prayer caught the worry
and turned it into a request. "Please guide him.

141

Bring people into his life that will help him understand your will."

When I chose to turn the worry into a request and acted on my choice, the peace of God— deeper than my own thoughts and feelings—peace that surpassed all understanding, kept guard over my heart and thoughts in Christ Jesus.

The tendency to be anxious, to pace in my head until I found a solution was still potential in me, but now I knew that I didn't have to act on that tendency. I could obey God's Word and tell the anxiety to him. I had a rule to follow: "Entertain no worry . . . under all circumstances let your petitions be known unto God."

Sometimes old habit pulled me into the brooding place again and I felt my way around in the dark. Hours (days?) later, I hauled the worry into the light again by speaking it in words to God and resting in his love. *I am the prodigal, Father. I have come to myself. I have returned.*

Now I understood: instead of keeping me *from* prayer, my human being tendency to worry could *become* prayer. "Anxiety . . . is intended to stimulate prayer" (Stuart Briscoe, *Bound for Joy).*

The stubborn part of my head wanted me to believe that the habit was too deeply ingrained— that I couldn't learn to tell my worries to God from now on and trust him for them. And that part of my head was right. But I *could* tell him this moment's anxiety and rest without being concerned about the next moment.

. . . In order for prayer to become an involuntary, or subconscious reaction to my problem, I must

142

*voluntarily and consciously practice it day after
day until it becomes an integral part of my being
(Billy Graham,* The Holy Spirit).

In the same way—continuously, moment by
moment—I could learn to tell God the other things
in my days. That way, prayer communion would
become a more natural part of my life.

Sometimes a problem was so serious that it
seemed to be threatening the Duckworth way of
life. Every morning when the day came into focus,
there it was, still unsolved. I'd tell it to God in
words, commit it to him, and thank him. There'd
be a hush, but soon *I have to know what to do*
buzzed in my head again until it had rubbed a
worn spot in my mind.

*What is God's will in this? Does he have some
action that he wants me to take? Am I being
irresponsibly passive by simply waiting? How can
I live peacefully in my new nature when my old
feels so unsettled?*

One day I sat at the sewing machine trying to
concentrate on the step-by-step pattern diagram in
front of me. "Why can't they write these things in
English?" But it was me, I knew. Part of my mind
was still circling the problem stubbornly, so that
my comprehension was poor.

I dropped the pattern piece I was holding, jabbed
the needle into the pincushion, and jumped up
with resolve.

From the bookcase in the living room I gathered
Bibles, a dictionary, a Bible dictionary; from its
place on my desk I took my journal. *Lord God, I
need to see this problem from your point of view.*

143

Guide my thoughts. Show me what Scripture has to say about it.

First, I summed up the problem and wrote it in my journal. Underneath that, I listed my initial insights.

Then, using a concordance and topical Bible, I listed passages that applied directly or indirectly. I used the dictionaries to look up words I needed to know more about. When a passage still wasn't clear to me, I brought in other translations, a Bible commentary, and an exhaustive concordance. In my journal, I wrote definitions and paraphrases.

When I knew, as nearly as I could, what a passage meant, I sat meditating on it before God. *How does this apply to my situation? What wrong attitudes are living in my head? How are my expectations distorted?*

As I rested and listened, the Teacher focused my attention on certain verses. My perceptions sharpened, my insights deepened, and I wrote what I was coming to see, in my journal.

Finally, I began to draw conclusions based upon the study and listed them in paragraphs. I knew that my knowledge on the subject was still incomplete and that the problem still wasn't solved. But I had hauled it out of the brooding place into the light. Intellectually I was satisfied because I had biblical absolutes on which to base my faith.

I spoke a formed-in-words prayer: "Thank you for giving me new insights into this problem. I realize that I know all that I can about it *at this time.* Help me to act on the things I've learned and to form these new attitudes. I commit the situation

to you. I trust you to show me what to do next.
I rest in you."

When the problem buzzed hot in my head again,
when I finally realized what was happening, I
stopped where I was. *I have worked through this
situation in your presence, Lord, and have all the
insight available to me right now.* Then, from my
will, I spoke to my old mind, "I choose to trust
you, God. To wait. To rest. Guide me further when
it is time."

Beneath my human nature, the peace of God
that surpasses all understanding guarded my
heart again.

At some moment in God's presence, I realized
that prayer without ceasing wasn't an age of grace,
a Pauline invention. Continuing prayer communion
had been God's design for man since the beginning.
"Seek the Lord and His strength; seek His presence
perpetually" (Psa. 105:4, Berk), the psalmist
reminded his people. I was only one of the historical
multitude who heard and was learning to obey.

FRUIT

13 Any moment that I abide in Jesus Christ, his attitudes are available to me.

The afternoon I was living in the Spirit of God as I stood at the shoe department cash register in J.C. Penney's, I loved the salesclerk (to whom I was "bedroom slippers, $6.95") with a smile and a word.

The morning I stood in the Spirit scrubbing mold from the shower tiles and a son appeared in the doorway asking, "Can you get out? I'm going to be late," I could die to my anger. *If he'd gotten up when I called him, he'd have been done in here long ago.* And, *Doesn't he even notice that I'm doing a dirty job to make his life better? He could show some gratitude.*

"Sure," I was able to say in love as I crawled out from between the toilet and tub to wait in the hallway. *I must be sure to remember to give him his lunch. Maybe tonight we can talk about his habit of sleeping in.*

God in me. God demonstrating himself through me. Instinctively, each time, I knew that this was the way a branch bore fruit.

It was midafternoon. A son walked into the kitchen, his face closed tightly, his words shut up behind it. One by one he let them out. "I . . . have . . . to . . . work . . . on . . . my . . . day . . . off."

He had plans. He was tired. His supervisor was careless when he made out the schedule. "I've had it. I've got a good mind to quit."

I became frightened because of his words. *Perhaps he'll walk off his job and be unable to get references.*

If I hadn't been swishing suds at the sink in fellowship with God, I would have countered with proper parental "shoulds" and "oughts." Instead, I continued to rest in Jesus Christ and spoke gentleness from the Spirit of love. "I know. It's hard to have to pay for someone else's mistakes." That gentleness was supra-Marion, a fruit of the Spirit of God.

During the years before God led me into intimacy, I hadn't understood what fruitbearing was. Did "Go out and produce fruit" mean the same as "Go, therefore, and make disciples of all the nations" (Matt. 28:19, Berk)? What about the Scripture that said, "The Spirit's fruition is love, joy, peace, forbearance, kindness, generosity, fidelity, gentleness, self-control" (Gal. 5:22, Berk)?

Not long after Jack and I were newly reborn, we met regularly to study Scripture with Florine, the director of Christian education in our church. We three sat in our living room reading Matthew chapter five in which Jesus teaches that the poor, the humble, the merciful are blessed. When we finished, she said, "Notice that Jesus isn't asking us to *do* something, but to *be* something." "Be-attitudes," she called them.

She led us through the thicket of our thoughts until we could see what she meant: that because we had the seed of God's nature, we could demonstrate his attitudes . . . and so learn to "be."

From a New York City apartment to Northwestern parsonages, I tried to be a Sermon-on-the-Mount disciple—to be little girl good and keep my hand clapped tightly over the rebellious part of me. I prayed for those qualities and waited to be filled forever. I memorized the verses that described the fruits of the Spirit while I ironed, as if the words themselves were seeds that would bud and blossom within me.

But the words refused to take root and grow so that I could hang heavy like late autumn with blue-ribbon love, joy, peace, forbearance, kindness, generosity, fidelity, gentleness, self-control. When a church board member bristled and pew people began taking sides, I prayed, *Help,* and shivered through the weeks as though *God* was a word foreign to my tongue. Only when I taught Bible was I consistently conscious of God's power in me. From the first time that I stood in front of a Sunday school class and spoke through a mouthful of cotton wool, I knew that I could depend on God to fill me when I taught Scripture.

I wanted to be more than an anointed worker sent to stand at the lectern, though. I wanted to *know* God the way the Apostle Paul said I could—with the "eyes" of my "heart" (Eph. 1:18, Berk). To be filled up with him so that I could minister godliness when the Fuller Brush man came while I was waxing the kitchen floor and my sons burst through the back door, leaving a trail of footprints in the wax while I was choosing a clothes brush from the salesman's catalogue.

During that period, I wrote in my journal:

November 30: At work, I read Thomas à Kempis on my break. I wondered what I'd say if the store manager who was working nearby, turned and asked me about what I was reading. I try not to stand out—to be discovered as a Christian. As I sat there, I wished to have a "religious" identity as Thomas à Kempis did, so that it would be obvious that I was a religious zealot. How much of my everyday silence is wisdom and how much is cowardice?

We moved from parsonages to a secular house with rent due on the first. I met Mrs. Lady down the street east and Mrs. Lady west and sat in their overstuffed chairs, smiling and talking neighborhood and listening to the holes in their conversations where God should have been. As we talked, I thought of Matthew's "Go . . ." and of John's fruitbearing branch and was ashamed. For I was only another Mrs. Lady with proper company manners, talking about my children and their children and last night's news. I demonstrated no greater-than-suburbia love that made them catch their breath, nor did I jump into the holes in their

conversations with God-words that brought them
low.

But while I was inspecting my branches and
mourning their barrenness, God the Gardener was
pruning me—at the store where I worked, at home
with my family during Sunday terror. Because I
had to depend on God to "be" in me in specific
ways, I discovered that I *could* depend on him that
way. I didn't have to see him in shining white
garments as I prayed or feel his presence so that
I could walk lightly over the top of my troubles.
Neither did I have to understand the John fifteen
principles of abiding, pruning, and fruitbearing.
Someday, up ahead, I will learn what they mean.

I didn't know it then, but every time I depended
on God to help me sell to strangers or make
popcorn during Sunday terror, I *was* abiding in
Jesus Christ as a branch in the Vine.

I learned to rest and sense God's presence,
and as naturally as the branch does it, I began
to bear fruit.

As I stood at the cheese board cutting and
wrapping wedges from a giant wheel of orange
cheese in the store where I worked, I heard
another employee's unusual silence and saw the
strain on her face. Sensing God's love, I spoke.
"How're things going at home? Any change in
that situation you were telling me about?"

She sighed and began to tell me the thoughts
that lay heavy inside her.

On another day an employee and I priced items
at the back counter. "How's the book going?"
she asked.

"OK, only I need time to give to it. This chapter seems to be taking me forever."

Then, because of God's love, I shifted the conversation from me and my things to her and her things. "It must be so hard for you to work here when you have small children at home. Don't you get frustrated?"

Still another day I walked up to the teller's window at the bank. She smiled a "Hello" and began tending to my business. An unusual pin that she wore caught my eye. I leaned into God and, instead of strictly business words in exchange for hers ("May I have it in five's and ten's, please?"), I loved her with my words. "What a lovely lapel pin. I haven't seen another like it!"

Perhaps I was the only one who noticed these meager firstfruits, but for seconds—like the click of a shutter—I could open up and smile or do God's love.

I was beginning to understand what Paul meant when he said, "Not I, but Christ liveth in me: and the life which I now live in the flesh I live by the faith of the Son of God . . ." (Gal. 2:20, KJV). The ability to show qualities of Jesus Christ—to bear fruit—came out of the nature of God in me.

On a visit to an old friend years before, I had sat across from her in her living room listening as she talked about her long-standing struggle to show love to a sharp-cornered Christian. The frustration and self-condemnation she'd felt creased her face and sounded in her voice as she leaned forward on the sofa and pounded the point with her words. "I tried and tried and kept failing because I was trying to do it in my own strength."

I nodded as though I knew exactly what she meant, even smiled slightly and narrowed my eyes with a practiced look of insight. But my mind was frowning.

"My own strength"? What does that mean? Physical strength? No, of course not. She means spiritual strength. But what is spiritual strength and how do you get it?

"In my own strength" was a cliche like the others spattered in sermons and used as fillers in religious magazines. "Let go and let God." "Stop trying and start trusting." They were slippery and slid in and out of my mind without leaving a mark. *Let go and let God—how? Stop trying and start trusting—how?*

This was a "how" that I couldn't figure out in my own head; God the Holy Spirit had to teach it to me. "Do this . . . and again. Now this. Again. Again." Off the bed with a push of determination and into family Sunday, praying silently, *You promised, Lord. "They that wait upon the Lord shall renew their strength"* (Isa. 40:31, Berk).

Life on the corner of Maple and Hickory gave me ample opportunities to practice patience or peace or the other fruits of the Holy Spirit. One such opportunity was during the summers when Mark played on Little League teams in uniforms lettered "Superior Tires" and "Salem Police."

Games began just before the dinner hour. "He can't play on a full stomach," Jack told me as I tried to plan meals. I knew he was right. "Let's all eat after the games," he suggested. "The family together."

So at nine at night (sometimes with the temperature still hovering around 90 degrees),

I was frying hamburgers; at ten I was scraping greasy dishes.

Seven the next morning I was back in the kitchen cooking the first of a series of breakfasts. Jack had to be at work early; John started later; Paul had the early shift but came home for a breakfast break midmorning.

We had conferences to determine the best mealtime schedule, but evenings after baseball usually found me in the kitchen. Old self whimpered for a budget that allowed us to eat out after games, and mornings for "just a little consideration." Every time, I had to choose whether to serve hamburgers and scrambled eggs with love or anger.

The more tired and frustrated I became so that something Adamic filled me up and fellowship was only light through the cracks, the more I realized that practicing the abiding disciplines consistently was the only way that I could show God's fruit and qualities.

. . . *The child of God who would master the final secret of the Holy Ghost, the secret of His constant manifestation, must* keep looking to Jesus *moment by moment until such abiding in faith becomes the constant attitude of his soul (James H. McConkey,* Three-Fold Secret of the Holy Spirit).

That was the principle God had been showing me that spring afternoon when I mowed and fellowshiped. If I practiced doing one thing at a time moment by moment in his presence, I could, for that moment, manifest his qualities and bear his fruit. Doing one thing at a time was a discipline that would help train my mind to consciously know that I was united with Jesus Christ now. The Holy Spirit would help me and gradually "abide in me and I in you" would take root.

Over and over those years I rediscovered the fact that the qualities of God are the fruits of the Spirit and they come out from his life in me moment by moment, for, as A.W. Tozer put it, ". . . Life is only a succession . . . of single, historical moments. No one lives his whole life at a time. . . . There is no other way to do it."

I was to practice the qualities that are natural to God's nature over and over, from moment to moment, as though patterning a new me. At the sewing machine, I practiced patience.

Since the eighth grade, my way with pattern and material was to cut it, pin it, sew it, and wear it—crooked seams and all. Now, as I sat to pin collar to back of neck, matching small o's, I sensed Tutor: *slowly, one step at a time. Sew in my presence.*

Was God really interested in the way I sewed?

He was. Everyday experiences—like sewing—were the ones God used most to teach me to live his way.

My neighbor, Marge, was an excellent, experienced seamstress, and I began to watch how she did it and asked questions. When a garment I sewed turned out ill-fitting, I asked for advice. "Did you make your seams five-eighths of an inch wide? That's what the pattern allows for. I still check my seams periodically, to see if they're right."

I went home to sew the way Marge did. *Slowly.*

*One step at a time. Preshrink material. Make
pattern adjustments. Set pattern pieces on fabric,
measuring to be sure it's evenly placed.*

Relax. Rest. Pin a seam. Baste it. Sew slowly.
Within, as I worked, I rested in the presence of
God, seeing the miracle of color, the feel of the
fabric, thankful for his provision.

Frying burgers after hours and performing
sewing tedium at the machine were opportunities
to train myself to abide in Jesus Christ moment
to moment and learn his ways.

During one of those "historical moments," I
hung the last pair of jeans on the clothesline and
stopped to inspect the tomato plants for blossoms.
Across the alley, a neighbor I'd never met was
lining her garbage can. She'd lived in her house
and I'd lived in mine; we'd waved and called
"hello" but never talked. Old self wanted me
to turn as though I hadn't seen her, pick up my
clothes basket, and go into the house. But words
with my neighbor were God's thing for this
moment. "Hi," I called and walked toward her.
"What do you think about this day?"

We talked for a few minutes about the late
spring and our gardens and then went back into
our own yards. I hadn't mentioned God's name,
but I had loved her in him. That, the Holy Spirit
confirmed, was the way I was to bear fruit for
that moment.

I began to anticipate next moments. What new
opportunity to demonstrate love would God give
me? I found one at the bus stop on the bench next
to an elderly lady clutching her grocery-filled bag.
"That looks heavy."

"It *is* heavy. I have to shop by bus now that my husband is gone. He died last year."

Later on the phone, I had an opportunity to bear fruit for that moment when I asked a friend, "Yes, but how are you *really?*"

I wanted to show love consistently to my neighborhood friends by beginning a Bible study in my home and sharing: *See? This is what Jesus Christ is like.*

For weeks, I trembled over the idea; it seemed to suggest an invasion of their privacy, as though I were to ask their bank balances or the states of their sex lives. But the idea persisted, gently, Holy Spirit fashion.

When I asked Jack what he thought, he said without hesitation, "Sounds good to me, if you think you have time to do it."

God does want me to do it! I had the desire in my spirit, confirmation by my mate, the ability, and opportunity.

The days ahead, I spent my anxiety by making plans: the study subject, format, a list of names of acquaintances who might be interested. A target date to contact them.

The day came and I stood trembling at the phone. *Help me, Lord.* I dialed. A friendly response. I dialed again. Most accepted my invitation for two weeks from Tuesday at ten in the morning.

For several years we studied Jesus Christ the incarnate Son of God weekly over tea in my living room. Our church backgrounds were as varied as America, but we came to agree that only personal faith in the Son allowed us to name ourselves

Christians. Weekly I sat in the big green chair with Bible and notebook spread on a TV table before me with my cup of tea, leaned into God in fellowship, and taught out of his love.

No more was my life divided into sacred and secular, ministry/non-ministry cubicles. *Sunday school at ten; God work.* "Anoint me to teach, Lord. Guide me to speak for you." *Bible class at two.* "Anoint me to teach, Lord. Guide me to speak for you." *Visitation on Thursday at three.* "Anoint me to visit, Lord. Guide me to speak for you," as though I were living in the Holy of Holies when I did church or parachurch work and with the throng in the outer court the rest of the time.

My body was the temple of God. If I were living in Love, ready to speak or do, all of my life was an offering—one moment when I talked with another mother at the Little League game, the next when I bought soda from her daughter in the concession stand. When I stood with the neighbor boy in front of the house as he showed me his gumball machine and watched proudly as I put in a penny and got a blue one "Just like mine," that was an offering and the next moment when I went inside to prepare a Sunday school lesson for my high school class, that was an offering, too.

When I used my gifts in the Spirit of Love and when I did human being things in him—both were ministry, though some might be of more eternal significance than others. "Let a man sanctify the Lord God in his heart and he can thereafter do no common act . . ." (A.W. Tozer, *The Pursuit of God*). For these acts to be from him, though, whether Bible class or luncheon salad—they had

158

to be done out of Spirit/spirit union. . . . "Being cast up into the moment-by-moment communion, personal communion, with God himself, and letting Christ's truth flow through me through the agency of the Holy Spirit (Francis A. Schaeffer, *True Spirituality*).

My responsibility was to live in fellowship with God and obey him; his was to bear fruit in and through me to his world. For as long as I lived I would have to submit to pruning so that I could grow in discipleship and produce more fruit. I'd have to deny old-self habits of impatience, fear, intemperance, pride, and practice their born-and-becoming antonymns. There would be no end to the opportunities I'd have to discipline my birthroom self so that it would exert less and less power over me. At the sewing machine, ripping and pinning and basting again, I could practice patience. During evenings at home with a book, when my head wanted cookies but my waistline didn't, I could practice temperance.

The times that Love lived in me, I realized that God hadn't led me into Spirit/spirit fellowship so that I'd use it up on myself. The purpose of abiding was to bear fruit. "My Father is honored in this, that you produce much fruit. . . . I have chosen you and appointed you to go out and produce fruit and that your fruit should be permanent" (John 15:8, 16, Berk).

God couldn't be contained in my human spirit. I had to allow him to flow out of me like Living Water. To contain him and love à deux would be less threatening to my born-and-dying nature, but that kind of relationship isn't compatible with the

159

nature of the divine. When I am living in the light as he is in the light and I sense mutuality with him, I know that. I want to show/speak/do love in an arms-around-the-world hug, but I know that arms-around-the-world is just a first, childlike response. I must define love to my world in concrete ways— by forgiving and bearing with and giving instead of receiving.

At the idea of sacrifice, my soul will be mortally grieved. I must be ready then to return to Gethsemane, to kneel and pray "My Father . . . as Thou wilt" (Matt. 26:39, Berk).

DEATH TO LIFE

14 I know now that I cannot die to sin and live in the Spirit by imagining myself nailed to a cross, entombed, and then rising to everlasting Easter mornings full of God. I can only die and live by abiding in Jesus Christ.

When Jack hands me a report to type full of figures to tabulate in precise columns and born-and-dying seethes, *Sure, sure, I suppose I've got to do it. If I don't, who will?*

Or I stand at the sink with a box of windfall apples, knowing that I'll have to dig worms out of their cores until the sink is piled with them, and born-and-dying storms, *Might as well recycle garbage as this stuff.*

Or family keeps interrupting when I'm trying to figure out how to resolve my latest manuscript problem. Or I must vote "no" when everyone else has voted "yes."

I know that if I turn away from born-and-dying and rest by faith in my risen Lord, I can die to

161

sinful responses and live in the power of the
Holy Spirit.

When I do choose to peel apples in fellowship
with God and at peace, I wonder as I pile worms
and peelings in the sink: *can this be the same
Marion Duckworth who sat in parsonages with
her Bibles and books while the washer churned
or the baby slept and tried to crack open the hard
Bible words "dead to sin . . . alive unto God"?
Who begged God over and over to help her
understand them?*

Sometimes at the sink over apples or at the
typewriter over a report, I remember *that* Marion
standing in front of an adult Sunday school class
at the back of a hundred-year-old sanctuary
smiling "hellos" down the rows.

My husband hadn't been pastoring in this church
long when they'd needed a new adult Sunday
school teacher. "I think you should teach it,"
Jack told me. It seemed right, so I took over.

The former teacher had been using a traditional
quarterly with verses and text, chalkboard diagram,
and memory verse for each Sunday. I'd been
teaching from it, expanding by using personal
experiences, insights, and related reference
material.

Lessons had gone well each week because
I'd been enthused about the subject and felt that
I had something to share that would lead to class
discussion. And discussion had begun, timidly
at first, but gaining momentum and depth.

One Sunday morning about halfway through the
series, after the last chorus in opening exercises, I
moved the lectern to position and stood before the

class. After marking attendance and exchanging teacher-student jokes, I began to teach.

The quarterly lay open on the lectern to the morning's lesson, "Death to Self and Life in the Spirit." My Bible was open to the Scripture: Romans chapter six.

The words didn't come out from inner Marion as they would have during a lesson on forgiveness that I understood and had experienced. I didn't understand these words, so I'd memorized them to recite as though they were Shakespeare and I was in the eleventh grade.

Whether or not the class discussed the passage, I don't remember. I remember only that the sanctuary seemed bigger, the empty space around me larger, the sound of my voice louder than it had ever been. And I remember the question that a woman about my own age asked: "You say that in order to die to ourselves, we must say 'no' to sin and 'yes' to Jesus Christ?"

I glanced at the quarterly. "That's right. 'No' to sin. 'Yes' to Christ."

She frowned and looked at her open Bible.

Back in the parsonage after church, I put my lesson book in the desk drawer and my Bible on the shelf and went to the kitchen. At the sink I dug my knife too deeply into the potatoes as I peeled them.

A son stood at the doorway. "How long till we eat?" I turned too quickly to answer and spoke too sharply.

Moments later, Jack was there echoing the same question. "I'm working as fast as I can," I snapped and turned back to thud pots and slam

silverware and insist without looking at his face,
"Of course nothing's wrong. It's just that you
people don't seem to realize that it takes *time*
to fix a meal."

Several years later on a day when I'd been
studying Romans six through eight until my head
hurt and my stomach ached from pressing to God
for illumination, I looked up and listened to the
steady conviction beneath my own thoughts.
"Stop. Don't study these chapters any more now."
I had sensed that conviction before when I
struggled to understand how I could die to sin,
but had pushed on anyway. *I must keep on until
I get it.*

This time, though, I closed my Bible and put
my books away on the shelf next to the ones I'd
bought for twenty-five cents at garage sales. *I
won't try to understand this any more. When
God is ready, he'll reveal it to me.*

For a long time I lived in an ellipsis, praying my
prayers and studying my Bible and teaching my
classes and wondering if I would ever understand
death to sin and life in the Spirit. Occasionally,
I read a magazine article on the subject and hoped
that it would be the one through which God would
shine illumination. This author's explanation was
worded differently; his illustrations were fresh—like
A.B. Simpson's words on sanctification: ". . . I
thought I had it. . . . Of course, it went with the
next sensation . . ." *(Himself)*.

There was a Scripture that had stood out from
the others one day when I read and prayed, as
though it were addressed "Dear Marion," and
signed "Love, God."

164

"Thus says the Lord, who made the earth, who created it, and who established it—the Lord is His name. Call to Me and I will answer you and reveal to you great and mighty things which you do not know" (Jer. 33:2, 3, Berk). "Things cut off, i.e., inaccessible, unattainable, or withheld." To Jeremiah the things cut off, withheld, had to do with the future of Israel. To me they had to do with Scripture's teaching on death to sin and life in the Holy Spirit of God.

When God did begin to reveal the life-giving principles that freed me from the control of the principles of sin and death, it wasn't by providing new, expanded Bible translations or more comprehensive commentaries so that I could see myself dead and alive and filled with Holy Spirit power over sin as I'd always supposed. *I'll be studying in my Bible and praying and all at once God will enlighten my mind. I'll jump from my chair and gasp in awe to God, "I see!" I'll understand crucifixion and resurrection with Christ and something called "death" will take place and I'll be filled full with him and able to live in his presence with power over sin.*

. . . It is something we are unable to do . . . The Lord Jesus Christ has come on purpose to do it, and (that) He will do it for all who put themselves wholly into His hands and trust Him without reserve.

The Lord's part is to do the thing intrusted to Him. He disciplines and trains by inward exercises and outward providences . . . He makes everything in our lives and circumstances subservient to the

165

one great purpose of causing us to grow in grace, and of conforming us, day by day and hour by hour, to the image of Christ (Hannah Whitall Smith, The Christian's Secret of a Happy Life).

When I stopped trying to *understand* the John fifteen words intellectually so that I could do them and waited to follow like Abram, I began to know without understanding *This is the way.*

. . . Believers . . . imagine that the Spirit, in teaching them, must reveal the mysteries of the spiritual life first to their intellect, and afterwards in their experience. And God's way is just the contrary of this. . . . We must live and experience truth in order to know it. *. . . True discipleship consists in first following and following and then knowing the Lord" (Andrew Murray, Abide in Christ).*

I sat on the front steps one Sunday afternoon early in my quest to die and live. We'd been to church and returned to eat our big meal of the week around the table. Jack's resignation from the missionary board with which we'd served was still fresh. He was looking for work and unable to find any.

"This is all I can give you for grocery money," he'd said the week before. "Make it last as long as you can."

Each purchase seemed to pose a crisis decision.

"Shall we keep getting the newspaper?"

"Hamburger is on sale. Should we buy extra for the freezer?"

One of our boys brought home the envelope of school pictures and looked hopefully at us. Another needed baseball shoes.

Fear of the future had stretched my nerves taut through the previous week. So after the dishes were washed and family dispersed, I stepped outside the walls that housed uncertainty.

As I sat in the sun, I could hear the sounds of family through the screen door behind me, reminding me of jobs and dollars. Why couldn't I learn to trust God? If only I could be dead to my disbelieving, anxious self and filled full of God.

Truth came rising from within. "You have already experienced death to self and life in the Spirit. Don't you see?"

Afternoon sun shone in my spirit. I *had* been able to deny my own feelings and obey God—at the store where I worked, sometimes at home with my family. Old anxieties weren't controlling me as often as they used to. *That is death and life, Lord? I see . . . I see! I commit myself to the process. Teach me death and life your way.*

By a thousand little mortifications and crosses, he did. Ego begged tender handling and when I refused and turned away to obey God's will for that moment, she moaned in real pain. Every time I chose to judge my own self-centeredness and turned humbly to God was a moment of scriptural death to life. The more I obeyed, the more sure I became.

I'd been thinking about the changes that had been taking place in me one afternoon as I worked at home, thanking God. As I walked from kitchen to living room, I remembered the ThD phrases that

167

I'd studied until my head ached. "Can I understand the theology of death to life now?" I wondered.

About four that afternoon I took down the books that I'd packed from parsonage to house with attached garage to the one on Maple Avenue, and spread them before me.

In the Bible I'd had since Jack pastored his first church, I turned to Romans chapter six. Pieces of the imitation leather cover were missing, a page ripped and taped, corners dog-eared. I read penned notes I'd made in margins and remembered the kitchens and bedrooms in which I'd struggled to understand.

"Knowing this. . . ." The words seemed warmer now, less intimidating. Many of them were still strange and fit awkwardly into my head. I opened the engraved covers of the frayed Jamieson, Fausset, and Brown commentary, careful of the yellowed pages that had loosened from the binding, symbol of my years of search. A sentence of explanation here . . . one there . . . were clearer now, and I smiled to myself.

For about an hour, I studied and made notes and asked myself theological questions about chapters six and seven that I couldn't answer. When it was time to mix biscuits for dinner, I rose easily to put the books away and went to the kitchen.

I hadn't understood much of the Romans theology, but still there was peace in my spirit. No aching head or stomach because I'd been searching inside the words for their secret meanings. *I have to get it so I can do it.* I knew that I was experiencing death and life by resting

in Jesus Christ and depending from moment to
moment on him even if I didn't understand
its theology.

Some months later Jack and I stopped at the
local Christian bookstore, a warehouse-sized room
lined with aisles of books, records, music, and
teaching aids. As usual, we separated at the door
with a word to "let me know when you're done."

I felt as I had when I was six and stood at the
candy case with pennies in my hand. "Which
shall I choose? McGee on Revelations? Jensen
on John?"

Then I saw it: *Romans, Word Studies in
the Greek New Testament* by Kenneth Wuest,
$3.95, paperback.

When Jack wandered only an aisle away,
I hurried to him. "Look! Just what I've been
looking for." I flipped open the pages and showed
him how the author carefully traced the exact
meaning of key words in each verse from Greek
to English.

That evening I sat propped by pillows on the
bed with Puppy curled at my side, a cup of tea on
the stand, Kenneth Wuest's *Word Studies* on my
lap, and Bibles and a notebook and pen next to
me. From his book, Mr. Wuest began to teach me
the precise meanings from the Greek of Paul's
words in chapter six. I read a page and then
another of definitions, interpretations, and
expanded translations, too excited to take notes.
*Later. First I have to run through the verses.
See them all.*

At each page, I praised. I woke Puppy up and
told her my joy. The bedroom was my seminary,

Mr. Wuest my professor. I read and he lifted old words from my Bible, unlocked them, opened them up, and exposed their meanings to me. With a mental switch, I clicked off the TV drama playing in the living room so that its sound wouldn't mix with Wuest in my head.

During empty places in other days I sat with *Word Studies* and compiled the meanings of the hard Romans words and their concepts in my notebook. As I filled pages, I began to understand that some of the deeper life phrases were built around words I'd never really understood—like "death." At the sound of its letters, my brain had automatically brought up its stored definition: *cease to exist.*

From Kenneth Wuest I learned that "Physical death is the separation of a person from his body, spiritual death, the separation of the person from God."

Death is separation! ". . . A cleavage . . . God used His surgical knife to cut the believing sinner loose from his evil nature."

That Sunday evening in my bedroom in Flushing, New York, when I had received Jesus Christ, God cut me free from my old birthroom nature—the one that had controlled me from my first temper tantrum—and gave me a new Christlike nature.

He hadn't tossed the old one into Gehenna, however. The Marion-centered nature that wanted to be praised and petted was alive and well and living in me. Now, though, I no longer *had* to wear it as if it were all I owned. Now I had a new nature. I was free to *choose* the one in which I would live.

Because of the Holy Spirit, I could "rid myself of the old nature with its previous habits . . . and . . . put on the new nature that is created in God's likeness in genuine righteousness and holiness" (See Eph. 4:22, 23, Berk).

I continued to study Romans from the Greek and absorbed more of its theology. *To "reckon" myself dead to sin and alive to God means to count constantly on the fact that I have been cut free from my self-centered nature and given a new God-controlled one.*

The power to live a Kingdom of God quality life was in Jesus Christ, second Adam, head of the generation of reborn ones. Every strength, every righteous characteristic was in him and was potentially available to my seedling born-and-becoming nature. Whenever I rested in that fact by faith, I was counting on the Holy Spirit to reproduce the quality in me.

Another of the blurred doctrines that came into focus was the identity of the "self" who was to "die"—the "I" who was crucified with Jesus Christ. Years before when my self-image was tottering and my sense of personhood undefined, I'd muddled over that biblical "I." *Which part of me does God want to do away with? Does he want me to lose my individuality and become filled with his?*

That "self" who was to die wasn't person Marion Duckworth, I knew now. God had created the baby my mother named Marion Sarah, unique to her voice and fingerprints. No face was exactly like hers; no one saw the world from behind that face exactly as she did. God loved this specifically created female unqualifiedly. He wanted Marion

171

Sarah, child of Isadore and Florence Maria, to walk his earth, feed his squirrels and finches aware that she was God's creation, that she was loved by him and to love him back.

The self who was crucified with Christ and who was to die experientially every day was my Eve-like tendency. Marion Sarah Siegel Duckworth had inherited her mother's nose, her father's curiosity, and the first woman's tendency to be disobedient to God. Everyone begotten by Adam and Eve had that propensity. Cain killed his brother; Abraham (friend of God!) dishonored his wife. My own self-centeredness was revealed in every stamp of my foot against authority, every idolatrous act, every narcissistic gaze, every scheming deviousness. I had come to identify that disobedient tendency within myself and to separate it from my personhood.

God didn't want to obliterate Marion Sarah Siegel Duckworth. He had come in Christ to sever her from the sinful bent that had warped her soul. She was reborn in Jesus Christ; she could rest in him, and die and live—day by day, moment by moment.

BY
FAITH
❉

15 The year in which I wrote the final
draft of this book was the most
difficult of my life.

Mornings I closed myself into
the writer's world that I had
created in my head. That world
was manageable. Papers I kept stacked in a pile at
my left. Dictionary, thesaurus, and Bibles were
lined in front of me. Adverbs and adjectives, nouns
and verbs might hide from me, but I would find
them finally and move them from here to there
where they blended with the ones alongside. A
sentence might stumble awkwardly across the
page, but I could erase the space clean and
create a new one.

In the world outside of my bedroom door, that
was not so. That world was crumbling. Some of
the people I loved were encompassed by troubles
like the strong bulls of Bashan. At times the
silence in our house was so heavy that I could
carry it in my hands.

In that world I couldn't erase the days clean and

create them new. So I stepped into each day resting as best I could in Jesus Christ and ate his promises like breakfast and dinner for strength.

By autumn the chapters almost formed a book. Midafternoons, I covered my typewriter and tucked the stray words into the back of my head for tomorrow, I put my books back in their places and stepped out of the world of words that I could manipulate into the world of circumstances that I could not. Jack and I were weary; solutions danced just out of arm's reach.

The troubles seemed to be moving inside me. I fell asleep at night but awakened a few hours later and stayed awake sometimes until dawn. I was growing tense, overly sensitive. I began to cry easily.

Finally, I made an appointment with the doctor for a calcium injection because I knew that under stress that mineral became depleted in my body. *Just a simple shot and you'll be fine,* I promised myself.

I sat on the examining table facing the doctor. "Squeeze my hands," he ordered holding them out in front of him. I squeezed. "Harder. Come on. As hard as you can." He shook his head. "You're losing your grip."

He tested my reflexes and kneaded my shoulders and spine. "You have all the physical symptoms of depression," he diagnosed and prescribed two weeks' medication, advising me to adjust the dosage to suit my needs.

"You need another prescription, but I don't know where you can get it filled." He paused. "You need good news every day."

He went on to salve me with stories about his
wife's chickens. "The red variety we've named after
characters from *Gone With the Wind,*" and then he
left me to smile over the idea of a rooster named
Rhett and a hen named Scarlett.

I walked the few blocks to the bus stop and
stood under the shelter. Sitting on the benches
were square-built elderly men and women,
probably outpatients from the hospital nearby,
wearing waiting-room expressions. Other days
I would have felt separated from them by vitality
and inner peace. Today, I was one of them.

But I'm not supposed to be like you, I told their
staring faces. *I know how to rest in Jesus Christ.*
A woman talked to me about the weather, and
I answered in kind and then turned within.
*Depression? Good news every day? But I know
the Good News. Why isn't that enough?*

The bus was late. People shifted and strained to
peer around the corner and asked one another if it
was coming yet. I maintained separateness from
them by silence. Even within, I had grown silent.

I turned away from the people and looked down
the long street that led back to town, to my house,
to my family; then I looked up into the clear,
undisturbed sky. The peace that it symbolized
settled into my mind and I turned to God in my
spirit. Born-and-becoming spoke loudly, *one thing I
know. The principles of abiding in Jesus Christ are
true. They are words from the mouth of the Lord
himself. The problem is not in the truth. The
problem is in me.*

For the next two weeks I took one-third of
one pill every twenty-four hours. At my checkup

175

I was pronounced well again and told to stop the medication.

For the next weeks I kept all these things and, like Mary, pondered them in my heart. After the writing day I canned tomatoes and thought before the Lord: *What went wrong?* I took long walks in the late afternoon sun and listened for insights. At night or in the morning I spread out the days of months before God and traced back to the beginning of that year.

Jack had been pioneering a new church out of state, coming home for a visit biweekly or whenever he could manage. Alone, I had faced every reversal before God. Kneeling by the sofa or bed, I let myself feel anxiety, listened to my real thoughts, and told it all to my Father. When all my resentments and fears, inadequacies and confusions were emptied out, I was ready to worship. God the present one filled my spirit, and like David's, my words changed from cries of misery to ones of praise and faith. From the Scriptures I read promises and meditated on them before him until they became my own. When I finally rose I was again face-to-face with the God who is peace.

I went to join Jack and in a few months we both returned to Salem to stay. As soon as we were together, without deliberately planning to do so, I began to shift the responsibility for wisdom, encouragement, strength, and stability during the unsteady times from Father to mate. *Now I can depend upon Jack to encourage me and solve the problems.*

I stopped meditating on God's promises until

they became my own, stopped spending extended
time in prayer, stopped pouring my feelings out to
God, waiting for him to mold my attitudes and fill
me with the Good News again. I still studied the
Bible and prayed as I always had. But my needs
were deep, and morning devotional time wasn't
long enough for me to show and tell God my
feelings and grow from fear to faith and intercede
for other requests, too.

Jack was supportive and sympathetic, but he
couldn't reach into my soul and heal it, nor could
he solve all our problems. I filled the Duckworth
table with food three times a day and tried to abide
in Jesus Christ, but I couldn't renew my mind
while I stirred the corn or sliced the bread. *I'll try
harder.* Still Marion within raged, so I tightened my
frame more firmly around my feelings according
to old Marion habit. Finally, I could tighten no
further, and found myself in one of the doctor's
examining rooms joined to the patients down the
hall by ailments and aches.

As I lived and worked before God, I realized that
I'd been refusing to own my humanity. I was a
spiritually reborn creature seated with Jesus Christ
in the heavenlies, but still, like the people who'd
sat with me in the doctor's waiting room, I was a
mortal. We mortals fall and break our bones and
inhale germs and come down with flu. We lose our
jobs and our way and sit stunned, unable to speak.
We look back at our dreams and ask why and try
to tell others how we feel but they can't hear what
we mean so we stare unseeing at the TV.

Eden creatures are flesh and nervous system.
Cut them and they bleed. Hurt them and they

weep. They respond to stress reflexively in their own peculiar fashion. Mine was by internalizing; others might scream invectives or kick the dog. We are humans, not characters ripped from a deeper life book.

This year I had lived through real stress and had responded in a fashion normal for a human being, child of Adam. I tensed to defend, argued *unfair*, and felt the days for a way out. For as long as I lived in flesh on earth, there would be times like these when I'd seem unable to live out of intimacy with God, to pray worries into requests and experience peace or think a "What'll I do?" problem through before him. Those times I would cry, "I am sinking in deep mire and there is no place for me to stand, I have come to deep waters and a flood overwhelms me" (Psa. 69:2). Rest would slip through my fingers; peace I would have left in my other suit.

The reasons would be multifarious. My physical and mental capacities might be diminished because of writer's burnout or an unwieldy body. Some internal shifting might be taking place that manufactured a list of symptoms, like this year's menopause. I might be measuring myself against Cathy, who sells real estate and is president of the Women's Club, and prod myself to move too fast again: *Things to accomplish. Money to make. This, then that, then the other.* People in my outer reality may have been jostled black and blue by ones in their world and have shoved their anger at me. "Feel my pain and pass it on." Or God might be dredging some half-submerged attitude from my soul in the ongoing process of death to life.

Those days I'll wake up angry because it's just another Wednesday. The sun will be too bright or the sky too gray. At the breakfast table, I'll clip my words short. My own feelings will make me feel guilty so I'll pray, but my feelings won't change. Jack will ask, "What's for dinner?" and my cells will tighten like fists. The lawn will seem all weeds and the kitchen all smudges and fingerprints.

Finally, because I am commited to follow Jesus Christ and the Holy Spirit is drawing me, I'll sink on my knees or into the big green chair—*Lord, I am in your presence*—and tell him exactly how it is with me until it is all told.

I'll review the days that have been like hell because I've felt as though I've been separated from God. *Satan?* I'll wonder. Has Satan seen my weakness and stepped in, stirring up my anger and discontent? Surely he is interested only in Job and Paul and Billy Graham. Then, slowly I'll remember that he is interested in me, too. Not for my own sake, but to hurt Christ and Christ's cause.

Whether I've been unable to experience intimacy with God because some physical ailment has left me feeling depressed, because of my response to Satan's temptation, some sin I have refused to own, or a combination of all three, I'll probably not be sure. I'll pray for insight so I'll be wiser next time and expect to understand further on. My body will be unwieldy and my mind obstreperous, but I'll rest in the presence of Father and meditate on who he is. Fellowship may be like hands in the dark until physical pain passes, my feelings subside, or God changes some born-and-dying attitude, but that will be enough to assure me that I am home again.

Haltingly, I'll begin practicing the abiding disciplines that God has taught me. It will be a weekday morning and about ten I'll need a break from the manuscript on which I'm working.

I'll get out of my chair and wander into the kitchen. *I'll do the dishes,* I'll decide. And, as I run water and squirt in detergent, I'll lean into the presence of God. *With you, Lord, this moment.*

I'll choose to feel the water on my hands in him, to wash each glass slowly, thankful for the one who drank from it. Moments will fold into one another, and I'll see the patterns and colors on plates as I rinse them and allow myself to feel secure in their familiarity.

As I confine myself to a moment with God, perhaps I'll swish my hands in the water and make bubbles or scrub a neglected pot bottom and give gratitude to God for grace as I do it. Once more, I'll wonder to God because, even in the worst times I can abide in Christ by moments if I choose to do so.

Back at the desk, I'll work and my mind will become occupied; when it is free again, I'll look back to Father and find that fellowship has been ongoing in that deep place called *spirit.* I'll practice his presence with my mind for moments, thinking my human being thoughts, knowing that *this is fellowship, too.* I'll become mentally occupied again, but still we'll be communing in the Kingdom place.

I'll succeed and fail and begin again. I'll know,

because God has been showing me, that I am not to become overly occupied with my success or failure to abide everlastingly.

Instead of wasting effort in trying to get into a state that will last, just remember that it is Christ Himself, the living loving Lord, who alone can keep you, and is waiting to do so. Begin at once and act faith in Him for the present moment: this is the only way to be kept the next (Andrew Murray, Abide in Christ).

My failures this past year have humbled me and caused me to sink my roots deeper into Jesus Christ. God has reminded me that to gain victory, you must have battles, some of which will end in defeat. I am thankful that he is faithful, even in my failures.

When I have been away from God and have returned, I want to explore every facet of our relationship as though I were running my hands over the face of a loved one. I sit in the kitchen on the floor sorting things and *hear* the music Paul is making on his guitar. I think love, and worship. *Thank you for sons.* I *see* Puppy's soft white belly and the pink nipples where babies could suck and wonder to God about his creation. I *know* him in the secret place of the Kingdom of God while I interact with others on this dying earth and I'm more sure than ever that Spirit/spirit fellowship is the best of all the lives that I could choose.

I wonder what hard things, what prunings, are up ahead, and in my imagination I experience the pain of new deaths to self. How many times will I

turn away from the Holy Spirit as though I cannot
hear, because I want to be done with pain?

I cannot live tomorrow. I can only practice
yieldedness and faithfulness during this moment
and leave tomorrow's tests with God. For now, I
rest in Paul's words to his spiritual son Timothy.
"I know . . . Whom I have believed . . . and I am
(positively) persuaded that He is able to guard *and*
keep that which has been entrusted to me *and*
which I have committed (to Him), until that day"
(2 Tim. 1:12, Amp).

I remember a small, Delicious apple tree in the
neighborhood that hung heavy with fruit in the fall.
The retired gardener who owns it had cared for it
lovingly, pruning it back low when its branches
were bare. He was in the yard when Jack stopped
to comment on its beauty. The gardener was
proud. "Help yourself. Bring a box and take all
you can use."

That fruit nourished us into the next year. But I
am not a tree or a grapevine to stand dumbly while
my nonproductive branches are pruned away. I am
a thinking, feeling creature with a free will who can
refuse to "endure for the sake of correction"
because I hate to be humbled and I am afraid to
stand tottering in my born-and-becoming nature
(See Heb. 12:7, Berk).

Because God does abide in me and has been
leading me into truth, I want to bear the fruit of
his nature more than I want freedom from pain.
Finally, I'll turn for pruning. I'll look around
frantically for a way of escape and then realize
that the way to endure is to rest in the Strong
Place which I know now is God in me.

In every moment I must count, not on my ability
to rest in Jesus Christ, but on his promise to abide
in me. My failures to practice the presence of God
and live dependently in him do not sever Vine/
branch life. I *am* in Jesus Christ. I have been one
with him since that evening in Flushing, New York,
when I knelt and prayed and was made alive in my
spirit. In a way that my mind cannot comprehend
but my spirit knows, I was in Jesus Christ when he
died on the cross and arose from the dead.

He, eternal Love, lives in me. Whether I practice
his presence or not, whether I obey him or not,
God still abides in me and I am still in the
heavenlies in him. My responsibility is not to *keep*
myself in him, but to count on the fact that I *am*
in him and to rest.

I know now that God doesn't mean for me
to hold the fact of his presence in my mind.
Fellowship with God takes place in the dimension
called "spirit" because God is Spirit, and can
continue even when I am mentally engaged. These
past years through the disciplines into which God
has led me, I have been learning that I can be
aware of my life in the Spirit while I live in the
world, and that I can allow that Spirit/spirit nature
to control me.

This past year there has been fire in the furnace
and burning on the soles of my feet. These haven't
been the soft, warm days of once-upon-a-time that I
could snuggle into and purr contented thank-you's
to God: *it's so good to be your child because the
bills are paid and the new furniture looks so nice in
the living room.* There has been no stability in my
external world in which to take my ease and no

promise of peace ahead so that it was *easy* to abide in Jesus Christ. This year I've been with God in the dark, begging for peace and ease and listening to his silence. *Your will,* I have prayed finally. *Pruning. More fruit. Much fruit. Your disciple.*

Day after day I have learned again that the rest of faith is not an existence like that of a jellyfish floating in the warm currents of the Gulf Stream. It is a series of choices to surrender and trust God completely that I must make from moment to moment. *I choose to rest by faith in your presence; to turn away from my Eve-like nature. I believe that I am in Jesus Christ and he is in me. That "the real life I now have within this body is a result of my trusting in the Son of God . . ."* (Gal. 2:20, TLB). *This moment I choose to trust in your life in me and to act on that choice. I will obey.*

Deep within, separate from my human being thoughts and feelings, is the one who is Peace and Power and Glory. We fellowship. It is the Sabbath in my soul.

Windows Live Hotmail

>
>

Want to race through your inbox even faster? Try th
free, too.)

SUGGESTED
READING

Briscoe, Stuart. *Bound for Joy.* Glendale, CA: Regal Books, 1978.

Brother Lawrence. *His Letters and Conversations on the Practice of the Presence of God.* Cincinnati, OH: Forward Movement Publications, n.d.

Duckworth, Marion. *The Greening of Mrs. Duckworth.* Wheaton, IL: Tyndale House Publishers, Inc., 1980.

Graham, Billy. *The Holy Spirit.* Waco, TX: Word Books, 1978.

Henry, Matthew. *The Quest for Communication with God.* Grand Rapids, MI: Wm. B. Eerdmans Publishing Co., 1955.

Hurnard, Hannah. *The Hearing Heart.* London: The Church's Ministry Among the Jews, 1952.

———. *Walking Among the Unseen.* Wheaton, IL: Tyndale House Publishers, Inc., 1977.

McConkey, James H. *Three-Fold Secret of the Holy Spirit.* Lincoln, NE: Back to the Bible Publishers, 1897.

Murray, Andrew. *Abide in Christ.* Fort Washington, PA: Christian Literature Crusade, 1968.

Nee, Watchman. *The Spiritual Man,* Vol. 3. New York: Christian Fellowship Publishers, Inc., 1968.

Ryrie, Charles Caldwell. *First and Second Thessalonians.* Chicago: Moody Press, 1959.

Schaeffer, Francis A. *True Spirituality.* Wheaton, IL: Tyndale House Publishers, Inc., 1971.

Simpson, A.B. *Himself.* Harrisburg, PA: Christian Publications, Inc.

Smith, Hannah Whitall. *The Christian's Secret of a Happy Life.* New York: Fleming H. Revell Co., 1888.

Tozer, A.W. *That Incredible Christian.* Harrisburg, PA: Christian Publications, Inc., 1964.

———. *The Pursuit of God.* Harrisburg, PA: Christian Publications, Inc., 1948.

Voget, Lamberta. "The Christian's Self-Prison." Chicago: Moody
  Press, 1960.
White, John. *The Fight*. Leicester, England: Inter-Varsity Press, 1977.
Wuest, Kenneth S. *Wuest's Word Studies in the Greek New
  Testament*. Grand Rapids, MI: Wm. B. Eerdmans Publishing
  Co., 1973.